Tools For Success
A Manager's Guide

Dr Suzanne Turner

THE McGRAW-HILL COMPANIES

London · Burr Ridge IL · New York · St Louis · San Francisco
Auckland · Bogotá · Caracas · Lisbon · Madrid · Mexico · Milan
Montreal · New Delhi · Panama · Paris · San Juan · São Paulo
Singapore · Sydney · Tokyo · Toronto

Published by McGraw-Hill Professional
Shoppenhangers Road
Maidenhead
Berkshire
SL6 2QL
Telephone: 44 (0) 1628 502 500
Fax: 44 (0) 1628 770 224
Website: www.mcgraw-hill.co.uk

Sponsoring Editor:	Elizabeth Robinson
Editorial Assistant:	Sarah Wilks
Marketing Manager:	Elizabeth McKeever
Senior Production Manager:	Max Elvey

Produced for McGraw-Hill by Steven Gardiner Ltd
Text design by Steven Gardiner Ltd
Cover design by Senate Design Ltd

McGraw-Hill

*A Division of The **McGraw-Hill** Companies*

British Library Cataloguing in Publication Data
A catalogue record for this book is available from the British
Library

Library of Congress Cataloguing in Publication Data
The Library of Congress data for this book
has been applied for from the Library of Congress

10 09
20 09 08 07 06
ANL

McGraw-Hill books are available at special quantity
discounts. Please contact the Corporate Sales Executive at the
above address.

When ordering this title, use ISBN 0-07-710710-1

Printed in Singapore

Contents

Contents

Preface

This book is a consolidation of many, many years of experience and hard work. Wherever possible I have traced the originator of the ideas and concepts, and duly acknowledged. However, many of these tools and techniques have been used in industry, taught in business schools in one form or another, for so long that tracing the original source has been a fruitless task. I would like to thank all of the people who designed and developed the concepts behind the tools in this book, and in particular those of you who it has been impossible to trace and officially acknowledge.

Acknowledgements

The road has been long and winding.

I have had so much help and support whilst writing this book, I cannot thank you all enough. Whether it be a generous smile as I walked down the street, a hug when the going got rough, or encouragement, faith and belief in me, it has all made a difference. Unfortunately there is not space enough to mention you all by name, but suffice to say I couldn't have done it without you all.

Some people have helped above and beyond the call of duty and friendship, so a big thank you goes to Zoe Storer, Angie Clarke, Rachel Burgess, David Leech, Julian Turner and David Alexander.

Someone once said everyone has a book in them. This book truly would never have seen the light of day without the help and inspiration of three exceptional people. Mum, Dad and Paul, I can never thank you enough. You made it possible.

Introduction

Who should read this book

The quick and simple answer is no one. This is one of the fundamental reasons why I wrote the book.

The pressures on managers are ever increasing, leaving them with less time and under substantial pressure to perform. This book has been written in direct response to a need vocalised by many managers and executives that we, at Potenza, have worked with over the last 10 years. What they were looking for was something of an executive summary on a number of management concepts that they could refer to. That is, concise and practical overview of useful business tools aimed at improving team and corporate performance.

So to return to the original question, no one should read this book; you probably haven't got the time. Instead, you should keep this book handy and flick through it whenever you need help with a problem, or a quick reminder of tools you have used in the past.

What you get

This book is the culmination of our experience in industry and consulting where we have used the various tools to deal with problems and explain ideas. Some of the tools are our own; many are from industrial and academic sources. What I have tried to do is present these tools to meet three objectives:

- To sort through the huge range of tools to find those that are actually useful in practice.
- To provide a balanced range of tools to cover a number of business issues.
- To present the tools in a format that enables you to find and use them quickly.

In doing this I have kept the academic descriptions to a minimum but have included enough information for you to apply the tool correctly. I have also listed key points to look out for based on our experience of using the tools. Finally, where appropriate, I have included templates and diagrams that you can photocopy to help when using a tool. Throughout the book, reference has been made (wherever possible) to the originators of the work and other useful texts to provide the reader with the opportunity for further research.

How the book is organised

The rest of this introduction covers a number of issues. Firstly, I explain the format that I have used to write each of the tools. Secondly, I list all of the tools on reference charts and explain how these charts can be used to find an appropriate tool quickly. The final part of the introduction discusses some general hints and tips, which are useful whatever tool you are using. The remainder contains the tools themselves.

Format of the tools

To make the book as simple as possible to use, I have presented the tools using a standard framework. Where possible, the description of the tool appears on a single page. If appropriate, the opposite page contains a blank example of the tool. This is intended for you to photocopy for your own personal use.

The various parts of the framework, used to describe the tools, are as follows.

Tool title

Fairly obviously, this shows the name of the tool. Unfortunately, many tools have been in existence for quite some time and consequently, they have been modified and adapted by a number of different people. Often, this has led to the same, or very similar, tools being given a number of different names. In these cases, I have used the name that is most representative of what that tool does, the index provides links from other names to the tools.

When to use

Of course, you are free to use whichever tools whenever you like. However, if you have not used a tool before, it can be useful to have an indication of when the tool is likely to be useful.

What you get

Again, to help you decide if a tool is likely to be useful, this section briefly describes the outcomes that you could normally expect.

Time

This section provides a rough indication of how much time is required to generate useful output from the tool. Of course, this can only be a guideline, as the time will vary depending on how the tool is being used.

Number of people

Again, this section is designed to give you a better feel for how the tool is used. In simple terms, it indicates whether the tool works best when used in a group or by an individual.

Equipment

The final piece of background information contains advice on the type of equipment that is useful when using the tool. This is to allow you to be prepared before using a tool.

Method

In this section the mechanics of actually using the tool are explained. Where possible, the methodology is broken down into a number of easy-to-follow steps. Although this section is concise, there is enough information to get you up and running.

Example

To further help you understand how to use the model, each description contains an example of how the model might be used.

Exercise

If after the description of the methodology and an example you are still unsure as to how to use the tool, you can try a simple exercise. Effectively, helping you to understand the tool by using the classical approach of *telling* you how it works, *showing* you how it works and letting you try it for yourself.

Key points

In this section I identify a number of key points to bear in mind when using the tool. Some of these points relate to the theory behind the tool. Most, however, relate to practical issues or problems associated with the tool.

Additional comments

This section contains additional information about the tool, such as its limitations.

Other information

In the final section I acknowledge the original work (where known) and where you can go to get extra information.

Hints (shown in 'file card')

Finally, I have included a number of additional hints to help you use the tools. These hints can cover a range of topics from alternative ways of using the tools to problems and issues to avoid.

How to find a tool

When I first considered writing this book my greatest concern was that it would remain usable and helpful. Based on our own experiences and discussions with practising managers, I realised that a key issue for 'usability' was being able to find the right tool for the job quickly. After trying a number of approaches for finding tools I decided to offer three methods to suit different requirements. The three methods are the Project Matrix, the Day-to-Day Matrix and the Index.

The Project Matrix

The Project Matrix recommends tools to help you during particular projects within your company. The left-hand axis of the matrix lists a number of generic project types. These are developing a business strategy, sales and marketing, manufacturing, customer/supply chain, quality, design, and information technology.

The top axis of the Matrix lists a number of generic stages within a project. Of course, all projects are different but, based on experience, most follow six basic stages.

The first stage is to define what the project is all about and to *define* its objectives. Once the purpose of the project has been agreed it is possible to start *analysing* the situation. When the situation has been fully understood it is possible to start to *create options* and alternatives to meet the objectives. Hopefully the project will create a large number of possible options. However, in practice, a company will not have the time or resources to adopt all of these options. Therefore, it will be necessary to *select* the most appropriate ones and then *implement* them successfully. Finally, it is important to *monitor and review* the success of the project.

The resulting matrix can be used in two ways. Firstly, if you have been assigned a particular part of a project you can use it to quickly find tools that may help you. For example, you may have been asked to select which initiatives should be used from a list created during a strategic planning exercise. In this case, you could refer to the box in the matrix that matches *Business strategy* with *Select options*. This box contains some numbers, one of which is 26. If you turn to Tool 26 in the book, you will see that this is the 'Effort Impact Graph'. This is a tool that might help you choose appropriate initiatives.

Secondly, the matrix can help you when you are undertaking a major project. For example, if you are leading a quality improvement programme you can refer to the *Quality* row on the matrix. Working across that row will provide you with a list of numbers for tools that can help you throughout each stage of the development of your project.

The Day-to-Day Matrix

The second matrix sorts the tools in terms of management issues that you might be faced with on a regular basis as opposed to specific projects. The categories used are as follows:

Analysis: These tools are designed to help you to analyse a situation. Some of the tools are numerical or financially biased while others are designed to promote discussion.

Creativity: These tools help to generate new ideas, solutions or products. They can be particularly helpful for looking at old problems in a new light.

Problem solving: This section lists tools that can help to create solutions to specific problems.

Communication: This section contains tools that help you to get your message across. Some of the tools provide specific guidelines for effective communication. Others are tools that I have found to be very useful in developing understanding.

Time management: These tools will help you to make the most of your time. Some help you to prioritise your efforts for maximum benefit. Others help to identify wasted time and effort.

Project planning: This section lists tools that can be used to help manage any type of project.

Improving efficiency: Many managers are concerned with improving the efficiency and effectiveness of their operations. These tools can be used to help analyse the situation and develop improvements.

External improvements: External improvements relate to making changes in areas outside of the main business. For example, working to improve relationships with suppliers or customers.

Sales and marketing: These tools are designed to improve your understanding of customers' needs. Additionally they will help you to review your product range and approaches to advertising, pricing and distribution.

Discussion points: Many of the tools can be used to generate discussion. The ones listed in this section are particularly good at creating debate leading to increased understanding.

Strategy: The final section lists tools that can help you to analyse your business situation and develop plans for the future.

To use this matrix to find appropriate tools, you firstly have to decide which of the categories best match your current need. You can then scan down the particular column looking for tools that have an 'X' in that column. These tools should be able to help with your particular situation. In most cases there are a number of tools listed in each column. Therefore, to further refine your search, you should look to see what other categories the tool is listed against. This will help you to spot the most appropriate tools.

For example, imagine you wanted to find a simple tool to help a team learn to solve quality issues within a manufacturing cell. You might decide that the most appropriate column is *Problem solving* and so look for tools listed here. As there are quite a large number, you should refine your search further. In this case, the fact that you want a tool for use by a team suggests that tools that aid communication might be useful. Equally, as the team is new to problem solving, they might need help in being creative in generating solutions. Consequently, you might look for tools that are listed against *Problem solving*, *Communication* and *Creativity*. A tool that meets all these criteria is Tool 16: 'Concept Fan'.

The Index

The final method of finding tools is for those people who are already familiar with specific tools, have been recommended a tool from another source or know the tools by other names. In this case you can simply look up the tool in alphabetical order in the index.

Tips on using tools

This last section of the introduction provides some basic hints for using the tools successfully. It has been designed for those users who have not had much experience of applying these techniques in practice.

Types of tools

Although there are a large number of tools included in this book, most can be classified as being a framework, flowchart, checklist, box, table, diagram or, a graphical tool and statistic. Each of these types is briefly reviewed below to help you select the right tool for your requirements.

Frameworks

These tools are the most comprehensive of the tools. They consist of a number of smaller tools that have been combined into a complete methodology that considers all aspects of an issue. An example of this type of tool is 82: 'Strategy Framework'. The main disadvantage of these tools is that they are less flexible than combining your own tools.

Flowcharts

These tools are similar to frameworks in that they provide a methodological approach to working through an issue. If you are new to working with tools, need to be consistent or simply prefer working in a structured manner, these tools can be very helpful. An example of this type of tool is 21: 'Customer Focus'. The 'step-by-step' method to describe how to use the tools is similar to the flowchart approach. The downside of flowchart tools is that some people find that they stifle their creativity.

Checklists

Checklist tools seem very simple in that they are usually just a basic list to work through. However, each list does capture the most important issues relating to a subject and so, working through it, minimises the chance of

making mistakes. These tools can also provide the basis for discussion within a group leading to greater understanding. An example of a checklist tool is 79: 'Sources of Innovation and Opportunity'.

Boxes

These tools are similar to checklists except that they link the issues to a number of other factors. For example, Tool 65: 'Product – Market Analysis' has axes of 'competitiveness' and 'complexity'. These axes are used to identify certain characteristics that are suited to a company. These tools are useful to help you think through and discuss an issue. They can also help you to explain your ideas to a group. The disadvantage of this type of tool is that they are normally highly simplistic and generalised.

Tables

Tables tend to be more complete than boxes and checklists. Again they encourage you to work through the most important issues on a subject but also often provide generic options or solutions relating to these issues. An example of a table is Tool 49: 'Manufacturing Benchmarks'. Unfortunately this type of tool can sometimes be too specific.

Diagrams

Diagram tools normally try to convey a particular concept rather than a detailed answer. They are useful for explaining new ideas to people and challenging preconceptions. An example of this type of tool is 87: 'Technology and People'.

Graphical tools and statistics

These tools are designed to process large amounts of data. Representing this data in a graphical format makes it much easier for most people to understand. Other statistical tools help you to make objective decisions about information and what it is really indicating. An example of a statistical tool is 63: 'Process Control Charts'. One concern with these tools is that they can sometimes distract from the real issues, especially if they are used without any real understanding.

Tools are there to help not hinder

It helps to remember that the tools in this book are tools just like those you use for DIY. In other words they are something that has been designed to make a job easier. For example, if you bought a new electric wallpaper stripper but found it harder work than using your old scraper, you'd take the new one back to the shop. You should use this mentality when using business tools. Don't feel forced to use some new 'all-singing' tool if it's actually making your job harder.

Different tools will suit different circumstances

As you can see from the earlier list, there are many different types of tools and they all have various advantages and disadvantages. Therefore it should be clear that they will more suited to certain situations than others. Returning to the example of DIY tools, hammers and nails do a great job at *attaching* bits of wood to a fence. However, they don't produce good results when *attaching* a mirror to the bathroom's ceramic tiled wall. The lesson is not to be surprised if a tool works really well on one project but doesn't seem to help as much on the next.

Sometimes tools work in ways that were unexpected

Sometimes tools work really well in a situation that they were not designed for. Have you ever opened a can of paint with a screwdriver? Again, all that really matters is that the tool is making the job easier. It doesn't matter if it's not designed to be used that way.

The tools can be used at different levels

On a similar theme, many of the tools can be used at more than one level. This is particularly true for the strategy and marketing type tools. For example, you can use Tool 91: 'Visioning – The Future' to look at industry in general. You can also use it to look at your department or to focus even further into your career. If it's helping you to understand what is going on, it's worth using.

Don't let the tools become the boss

Another important point to remember when using any of the tools is that they can never tell you *not* to do something. Rather they can highlight areas where there might be more risk or where you are attempting something unusual. It is then your job to decide if the risk is acceptable or whether it can be reduced to acceptable levels. The tools are best at raising issues and encouraging appropriate discussion.

Everyone has different preferences

Just as the tools work better or worse in certain circumstances, so they will work better or worse with different people. It is important to remember this when working with groups. In particular you shouldn't try to force a group to use a tool just because you like it. If it is making their job more difficult try something else.

■ Using this book

The main message from this section is that you are more likely to have the right tool for the job if you have a large number of tools to choose from. The good news is that, now you've got this book, you have. So try to keep the book somewhere handy and don't be afraid to pick it up and scan through it when working on a problem. If it provides a tool that helps you get the job done, then great. Of course, it's even easier if you are familiar with the tools and only need the book for occasional reference. So why not get into a routine of working through the examples of tools that are suited to your circumstances? This *practice* will then pay off when you need the tool for real.

Anyway, thanks for buying the book. I hope you find it interesting, exciting and fun to use. I am confident that if used with intelligence and sensitivity it will enable you to transform the performance of yourself, your team and your company.

I look forward to hearing from you and enlisting your support to develop the cause of this book.

To you and your success.

Dr Suzanne Turner
S.Turner@potenza.co.uk

The Project Matrix

Project type	Stage					
	Define objectives	Analyse situation	Create actions	Select options	Implementing change	Monitor and review
Business strategy	2, 3, 5, 9, 15, 36, 42, 43, 50, 57, 71, 75, 79, 81, 82, 85, 86, 87, 91	2, 3, 10, 12, 14, 15, 22, 27, 30, 31, 43, 44, 57, 65, 66, 67, 68, 71, 74, 77, 81, 83, 84, 88, 89, 91	1, 2, 4, 7, 16, 32, 47, 54, 56, 58, 68, 71, 79, 81, 91	5, 6, 23, 26, 33, 61, 70, 71, 78, 81, 82, 91	2, 11, 12, 13, 18, 21, 34, 40, 41, 48, 53, 71, 80, 91, 94	2, 6, 12, 14, 17, 19, 20, 35, 40, 51, 52, 57, 69
Sales and marketing	2, 5, 7, 9, 36, 42, 43, 45, 46, 50, 75, 81, 85, 87, 91	2, 3, 5, 7, 10, 12, 14, 22, 25, 27, 28, 29, 30, 31, 38, 43, 44, 57, 64, 65, 66, 67, 74, 77, 83, 84, 88, 89, 92	1, 4, 5, 6, 7, 16, 25, 32, 47, 54, 56, 59, 64, 66, 79, 93	5, 6, 7, 23, 26, 33, 61, 62, 70, 78, 82	7, 11, 12, 13, 18, 21, 34, 39, 40, 41, 48, 53, 80, 94	2, 6, 12, 14, 17, 19, 20, 35, 38, 40, 51, 52, 58, 69, 72, 73
Manufacturing	2, 9, 36, 42, 43, 47, 49, 55, 75, 82, 85, 86, 87, 91	2, 3, 7, 10, 12, 22, 27, 28, 29, 30, 31, 37, 38, 43, 44, 49, 55, 57, 64, 77, 83, 84, 88, 89, 92	1, 4, 7, 16, 24, 32, 47, 49, 54, 55, 56, 64, 89, 93	6, 7, 23, 33, 55, 62, 70, 78, 82	7, 11, 12, 13, 18, 21, 34, 39, 40, 41, 48, 53, 55, 80, 94	2, 6, 12, 17, 19, 20, 35, 38, 40, 51, 52, 55, 58, 63, 69, 72, 73
Customer/Supply chain	2, 5, 9, 36, 42, 43, 45, 46, 47, 75, 82, 85, 86, 87, 91	2, 3, 5, 7, 10, 12, 14, 22, 27, 28, 29, 30, 31, 37, 38, 43, 44, 57, 54, 74, 77, 83, 84, 88, 89, 92	1, 4, 5, 7, 8, 16, 32, 47, 54, 58, 59, 64, 66, 79, 93	5, 6, 7, 8, 23, 26, 33, 62, 70, 78, 82	7, 8, 11, 12, 13, 18, 21, 34, 39, 40, 41, 48, 53, 80, 94	2, 6, 12, 14, 17, 19, 20, 35, 38, 40, 51, 52, 58, 63, 69, 72, 73
Quality	2, 9, 24, 36, 42, 43, 47, 68, 75, 76, 82, 85, 36, 87, 91	2, 3, 7, 10, 12, 22, 24, 27, 28, 25, 30, 31, 37, 38, 43, 44, 57, 64, 68, 76, 77, 83, 84, 88, 89, 92	1, 4, 7, 16, 24, 32, 47, 54, 55, 64, 76, 79, 93	6, 7, 23, 24, 26, 33, 62, 70, 76, 78, 82	7, 11, 12, 13, 18, 21, 34, 39, 40, 41, 48, 53, 76, 80, 94	2, 6, 12, 17, 19, 20, 35, 38, 40, 51, 52, 58, 63, 69, 72, 73, 76
Design	2, 9, 36, 42, 43, 47, 75, 82, 85, 86, 87, 91	2, 3, 7, 10, 12, 22, 27, 28, 29, 30, 31, 37, 38, 43, 44, 57, 64, 77, 83, 84, 85, 89, 92	1, 4, 7, 16, 24, 32, 47, 54, 54, 56, 64, 79, 93	6, 7, 23, 26, 33, 62, 70, 78, 82	7, 11, 12, 13, 18, 21, 34, 39, 40, 41, 48, 53, 80, 94	2, 6, 12, 17, 19, 20, 35, 38, 40, 51, 52, 58, 63, 69, 72, 73
Information technology	2, 9, 36, 42, 43, 47, 75, 82, 85, 86, 87, 91	2, 3, 7, 10, 12, 22, 27, 28, 29, 30, 31, 37, 38, 43, 44, 57, 64, 77, 83, 84, 88, 89, 92	1, 4, 7, 16, 32, 47, 54, 56, 64, 79, 93	6, 7, 23, 26, 33, 62, 70, 78, 82	7, 11, 12, 13, 18, 21, 34, 39, 41, 48, 53, 80, 94	2, 6, 12, 17, 19, 20, 35, 38, 40, 51, 52, 58, 63, 69, 72, 73

The Day-to-Day Matrix

Number	Tool	Analysis	Creativity	Problem solving	Communication	Time Management	Project Planning	Improving Efficiency	External Improvements	Sales and Marketing	Discussion Points	Strategy
1	Analogies – Creative Problem Solving	X	X	X	X							X
2	Balanced Scorecard						X	X	X			X
3	Benchmarking	X						X	X	X	X	
4	Brainstorming	X	X	X								
5	Brand Development				X					X	X	X
6	Breakeven Analysis	X					X					
7	Business Design and Improvement	X						X	X			
8	Business Ethics								X		X	
9	Business Excellence Framework	X		X	X		X	X	X		X	X
10	Cause and Effect Analysis	X						X				
11	Change Cycle	X		X	X			X			X	
12	Climate for Change Indicator	X			X			X	X		X	
13	Communication				X			X			X	
14	Competitive Product Placement				X					X	X	X
15	Competitor Analysis				X						X	X
16	Concept Fans		X	X	X							
17	Creating a Financial Business Case	X					X					
18	Creating Commitment						X	X			X	
19	Critical Path Analysis	X				X	X	X				
20	Cultural Audit	X						X			X	
21	Customer Focus	X					X	X	X		X	X
22	Decision Mapping	X						X			X	

#	Technique							
23	Decision Tables	X				X		
24	Design of Experiments			X		X	X	
25	Diffusion of Innovation					X	X	
26	Effort Impact Graph	X		X		X		
27	External Analysis (PEST)	X			X	X		X
28	Failure Mode Effects and Criticality Analysis	X		X		X		
29	Fault Tree Analysis	X		X		X		
30	Five Whys	X		X		X	X	
31	Flowcharting	X	X					
32	Forced Combinations	X	X	X				
33	Forced Pair Comparison	X						
34	Force Field Analysis	X		X		X		
35	Forward Measurement	X				X		
36	Gantt Chart				X			
37	Hazard and Operability Studies	X		X		X		
38	Histograms	X						
39	House Keeping – 5S				X	X		
40	Improvement Cycle			X		X		
41	Improving Group Communication	X		X		X	X	
42	Influence and Control	X		X	X	X		
43	Influence Diagrams	X		X				
44	Input Output Analysis	X		X		X		
45	International Business Context			X	X			
46	International Etiquette			X	X			
47	Just In Time (JIT)			X	X	X		
48	Learning Styles	X		X		X	X	
49	Manufacturing Benchmarks	X				X		
50	Marketing Mix	X			X	X		X

The Day-to-Day Matrix (cont.)

Number	Tool	Analysis	Creativity	Problem solving	Communication	Time Management	Project Planning	Improving Efficiency	External Improvements	Sales and Marketing	Discussion Points	Strategy
51	Measurement and Accountability	X						X			X	
52	Measurement Guidelines							X			X	
53	Meeting Management				X	X		X				
54	Networking				X	X		X	X	X		
55	Optimised Production Technology (OPT)	X						X	X			
56	Option Generation		X								X	X
57	Order Qualifiers and Order Winners	X							X			X
58	Pie Diagrams	X			X							
59	Power Maps	X			X			X		X	X	
60	Presenting – Communication				X	X					X	
61	Pricing Strategies									X	X	X
62	Prioritisation Matrix					X		X				
63	Process Control Charts			X	X			X	X			
64	Process Mapping – IDEF	X		X				X				
65	Product – Market Analysis	X									X	X
66	Product – Market Strategy Analysis	X									X	X
67	Product Life Cycle				X		X				X	X
68	Quality Functional Deployment (QFD)	X						X	X			X
69	Radar Chart	X			X			X				
70	Risk Management	X						X			X	
71	Road Mapping		X				X	X				X
72	Run Chart	X										

#	Technique
73	Scatter Diagram
74	Scenario Planning
75	Shared Values
76	Six Sigma
77	Skills Matrix
78	Solution Effect Analysis
79	Sources of Innovation and Opportunity
80	Stakeholder Analysis
81	Strategic Planning
82	Strategy Framework
83	SWOT Analysis
84	Systems Thinking
85	Team Selection
86	Team Working
87	Technology and People
88	Thought Capture
89	Time Based Process Mapping (TBPM)
90	Time Management
91	Visioning – The Future
92	Vital Few Analysis
93	Waste Minimisation
94	Work Package Breakdown

The Tools

1

Analogies – Creative Problem Solving

When to use
When looking for alternative, creative views on a situation or subject.

What you get
A fresh look at the issues from a different perspective.

Time
Half-an-hour to about 2 hours normally provide a useful output.

Number of people
1–15 people, groups of more than five normally produce a better outcome.

Equipment
Somewhere to capture the developments, a wipe board or flip chart.

Method
1 Clearly define the issue that you are considering.
2 Identify an analogy between the issue and another issue that everyone understands.
3 Discuss the issue that everyone understands.
4 Compare the solutions/ideas and translate them back to the original issue.

   If an analogy is not forthcoming, you could use a word drawn at random from a dictionary. Base your analogy on that word.

5 Build on the findings to create actions.

Example
Problem: Product introduction needs to be faster.
Analogy: Product introduction is like breaking the four-minute mile.

Relating the ideas back to the original problem.

Exercise
Consider your vision of the future of your business using the analogy of 'transportation'.

Key points
Using pictures also adds to the creativity of the ideas generated.

It is important that people get into the spirit of things – ensure the people involved are prepared to trust the process.

Don't try and shoehorn reality into an analogy. If it doesn't work, use more than one to capture all of the aspects, e.g. use the four-minute mile and the moon landing.

Additional comments
If people are not into the spirit of things, it will be difficult to get value out of the exercise.

▨ Other information

There are many books on creative thinking, some useful ones are:

E. DeBono, *Serious Creativity*, HarperCollins, 1994; R. Von Oech, *Creative Whack Pack*, US Games Inc., 1989; M. Michalko, *Cracking Creativity*, 10 Speed Press, 1998; B. Mattimore, *99% Inspiration: Tips, Tales and Techniques for Liberating your Business Creativity*, AMACOM, 1993.

2

Balanced Scorecard

When to use
When wanting to translate a vision or strategy into specific measures and goals.

What you get
A picture of business performance relative to the vision and strategy in four main areas or 'perspectives': financial, internal, learning/growth and customer.

Time
To initially set up a balanced scorecard can take up to 2 months – this time will be significantly reduced if elements such as strategy and vision already exist. Once set up it is an ongoing health check on the business and will need to become part of people's everyday jobs.

Number of people
For the initial set up about 15.

Equipment
Wipe board, flipchart, somewhere visible to display the scorecard.

Method
1 Define the industry, its development and the role of the company – consider this in the timeframe – yesterday, today and tomorrow. Useful tools are: 83: SWOT Analysis; 56: Option Generation; 27: External Analysis (PEST).

2 Establish or confirm the company's vision and strategy. Useful tools can be found under Strategy on the Day-to-Day Matrix.

3 Identify the perspectives for measurement that are clear and understandable for your business. The original model uses four: financial, internal, learning/growth and the customer. Others may be added, for strategic reasons.

4 Break the vision down according to each perspective and formulate overall strategic aims. Use the table shown on the page opposite as a guide.

5 Identify the critical factors for success.

6 Develop realisable measures with which to evaluate these factors. Consider carefully the interactions between the measures, Tool 84: Systems Thinking provides a useful method. Also to identify any potential knock-on effects of the measures, there is value in putting each one through a Tool 78: Solution Effect Analysis.

7 Analyse the measures as a whole to ensure they provide a 'balanced' picture.

8 Establish a comprehensive, top-level scorecard and gain approval in the organisation (you may be required to provide background to the scorecard's development).

9 Take the top-level scorecard and create more detailed cards throughout the organisation, translating strategy down to day-to-day tasks.

10 Formulate goals for every measure used. Ensure that there are both short- and long-term goals.

11 Develop an action plan to achieve the goals and strategy that have been set. Prioritisation will be key.

12 Continuously review, use as a dynamic functioning part of people's daily jobs.

Example

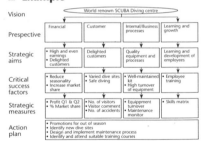

Adapted and reprinted by permission of *Harvard Business Review*. Exhibit from 'Putting the balanced scorecard to work; by R. S. Kaplan and D. P. Norton, September–October 1993, p. 139. Copyright © 1993 by the Harvard Business School Publishing Corporation, all rights reserved.

Exercise
Develop a high-level balanced scorecard for a supermarket.

Key points
The process of developing a scorecard is as valuable as the scorecard itself.

Companies should not try and shoehorn existing measures into the scorecard; they must take a new look at the business and develop both financial and non-financial measures accordingly.

Viewing the company from different perspectives and different time dimensions provides a unique understanding of the business.

Linking strategy to actions and measuring this on both a financial and non-financial basis provides a more balanced approach to business development.

▦ **Other information**

Concept developed by R. Kaplan and D. Norton, *Translating Strategy into Action, The Balanced Scorecard*, HBS, 1996. For a practical guide see N. Olve, J. Roy and M. Wetter, *Performance Drivers, A Practical Guide to Using the Balanced Scorecard*, Wiley, 1999.

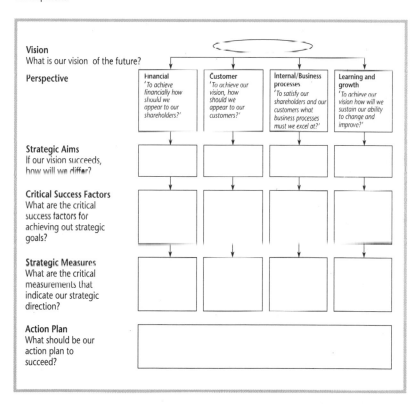

3

Benchmarking

When to use

If you are interested in learning, from other organisations, ways to improve your own organisation.

What you get

A disciplined approach to assessing and improving the performance of the business in critical areas.

Time

To do properly it requires substantial investment of management effort. This is because it is a continuous process and, to benefit from it, changes must be made as a result of the findings.

Number of people

This will vary depending on the scope of the study. As a general rule, it is worth involving a broad selection of people.

Equipment

Somewhere to visibly display the findings.

Method

1 Define
   a. Select the area to be studied.
   b. Define the process that is to be benchmarked.
   c. Identify potential benchmarking partners.
   d. Identify the data required, sources and appropriate methods of collection.

   > They do not have to be from the same industry as you, and in some circumstances it is more advantageous to look further afield.

2 Analyse
   a. Collect the data and select benchmarking partners.
   b. Determine the performance gap.
   c. Establish the difference in the process.
   d. Target future performance.

3 Implement
   a. Communication and commitment.
   b. Adjust targets and develop improvement plan.
   c. Implement and monitor
4 Review progress and recalibrate.

There are a number of different ways in which this process can be followed; the table highlights some of the trade-offs that need to be considered before embarking on a benchmarking exercise.

In-house comparison	Third-party comparison
Less likely to yield proprietary information	Likely to yield proprietary information
Benefits of first-hand observation	Indirect observation therefore objective data
Generally lower cost	Generally higher cost
Service or company sponsored	**Profession sponsored**
Tailored focus	Multi-focused
Shorter duration	Longer duration
Higher cost	Lower cost

Example

Ways to conduct benchmarking:
Direct exchange: Written questionnaires, phone surveys, teleconferences and video link, interviews.
Site visits: Validations and extension of concepts.

Exercise

Benchmark your favourite sports team. Remember that its performance is unlikely to be due solely to the ability of individuals. Instead it will be a combination of individuals' ability, teamwork, the tactics used and other factors.

Key points

Benchmarking is an ongoing process for continuous improvement.

Benchmarking Code of Conduct – '*Never ask for something you would not be prepared to share in return*'.

Additional comments

It is important not just to meet the standards but exceed them in critical areas of the business in order to truly gain competitive advantage.

■ Other information

Developed from, and for further information, see: S. Codling, *Best Practice Benchmarking*, Gower, 1995; S. Codling, *Best Practice Benchmarking – An International Perspective*, Gulf Publishing Company, 1996; S. Codling, *Benchmarking*, Gower, 1998; http://www.benchmarking.co.uk.

Stage	Explanation
Define	
Select the area to be studied.	Think about what your customers want from the business. What are the issues that are likely to attract and retain business today and in the future? These are the areas that you need to excel at.
Define the process that is to be benchmarked.	Think about those processes that really make an impact on the area to be studied. Think about the parts of the business that add value for the customer.
Identify potential benchmarking partners.	Who is the best in your industry? Who is regarded as being world-class in this area? Are there companies in other industries with a reputation for excellence? Have a look at: www.benchmarking.co.uk who offer consultancy and services in this area or www.benchnet.com.
Identify the data required, sources and appropriate methods of collection.	Brainstorm ideas for the type of data that you can collect to measure the performance of your own and the benchmark company. Trade fairs, journals, newspapers, customer surveys, etc. can all be alternatives to collecting data directly from the benchmark company. Be creative!
Analyse	
Collect the data and select benchmarking partners.	From all of the ideas created during the Define stage, you need to evaluate the various options. Take into account factors such as the quality of the data, the cost and time involved in collecting it and whether you are prepared to share data with other companies.
Determine the performance gap.	Make honest comparisons between your performance and that of the benchmark companies. You need to identify areas where there is significant room for improvement and also that will contribute to business success.
Establish the difference in the process.	Once you know the areas to be improved you will need to examine the benchmark company in more detail. Dig beneath the data to understand what they are really doing better than you and, more importantly, *how* they are doing it.
Target future performance.	Once you have understood the potential for improvement you need to develop realistic targets for internal development projects.
Implement	
Communication and commitment.	The data collected during the analysis stage can be used to convey the scale of the problem and potential for improvement. This can help to create acceptance and commitment to the process of improving.
Adjust targets and develop improvement plan.	Individual improvement projects should be established to address the areas for improvement. Plans and targets for these projects should be developed by the people who will be running them, not necessarily the benchmarking team.
Implement and monitor.	There is no point in benchmarking if you are not going to make improvements. Therefore you need to implement any changes and monitor them to make sure they are achieving what you expected.
Review	
Review progress and recalibrate.	Unfortunately the 'best' in business is constantly getting better. Hopefully your performance will be improving too. However, to get the most out of benchmarking, it should be an ongoing process.

4

Brainstorming

When to use
When an issue or problem would benefit from the fast collection of creative 'group think'.

What you get
A wide variety of ideas in a short space of time. Based on the concept: 'The best way to have a good idea is to have lots of ideas'.

Time
From 15 minutes to 1 hour.

Number of people
For best results 3–20 people.

Equipment
Somewhere to visibly display the ideas that are generated. It is also worth having the rules of brainstorming visible. The rules are on the page opposite. It is important that they are enforced.

Method
1 Clearly state the problem or topic and make sure everyone understands.

> When the ideas dry up it is time to stop.

2 Ask each team member to present his or her ideas, one at a time, in sequence (team members can pass if they don't have an idea).

3 Record all of the ideas exactly as given. No judgements are made until the end of the session.

> This is particularly useful if there are different levels of confidence in the group, as it allows the quieter ones to put forward their ideas, and prevents the louder ones from taking over. It is possible to run it with the ideas just free flowing.

4 After all of the ideas are listed, check for clarification by the team member.

5 The group then examines each idea in turn, expanding them and perhaps combining or eliminating some.

6 It may be possible to then group the ideas and put them under headings, which can then be used as key areas to take forward.

> Put time limits on gaining consensus to prevent creating a 'talking shop'.

Exercise
Brainstorm ways to improve your business.

Additional comments
There are a number of different ways to run brainstorming sessions in addition to the one described in point 2 above, however, the rules remain the same.

With Post-its™: Everyone writes as many ideas as they can think of about the specified topic or problem on separate Post-it™ notes. These are then stuck on the wall for the whole group to see. The Post-its are then grouped by subject or headings.

For a large group: If you want to consolidate ideas from a large group it is also possible to run it in subgroups. In a similar way to the Post-it™ note version, each individual brainstorms the key issues and captures them. These ideas have to be then shared with someone else and a consensus has to be reached as to the most important points (ideally about five points). These (five) most important issues are then shared with another group and again consensus as to the (five) most important has to be reached. This process of combining the important few from two groups and then selecting the most important to go forward is continued until the whole group combines to agree on the most important issues.

Using pre-work: Sometimes it can be useful to ask people to brainstorm an idea *before* they get together in a session. This enables the more methodical thinkers the time they may need to think through an issue. Everyone's ideas can be combined and developed as per stages 5 and 6 of the method.

Other information
Concept originates from Alex Osborn, 1953.

RULES FOR BRAINSTORMING

During idea collection

- No criticism
- 'Free-wheeling' welcome
- Quantity is needed
- No questions during session
- State ideas quickly
- No enlargement needed
- Don't mind stating the obvious
- Don't fear repetition
- Combine and improve on others
- Don't fear repetition

During the assessment phase

- Only criticise the idea, not the person

5

Brand Development

■ When to use
When developing your company's brand as part of a marketing strategy.

■ What you get
A framework around which the brand can be developed.

■ Time
To develop the framework will take about half a day, the research and actions that result will take substantially longer.

■ Number of people
Ideally, 9–20 people, including a wide cross-section from customers, suppliers and across the business to provide a balanced perspective.

■ Equipment
Somewhere to capture the output.

■ Method
1 Identify all of the groups of people who are touched by the branding. Tool 80: Stakeholder Analysis or Tool 4: Brainstorming, would help here. Group the stakeholders into like mindsets.
2 Consider what image you want these people to have of the company or product. These will include tangible and intangible elements. For example, quality, feel good, environmentally friendly, safe, value. Group the factors into manageable sets.
3 Carry out some research in each of the stakeholder groups to understand where the brand currently rates on each of the issues.
4 Plot the findings against the ideal brand image that you are looking for from stage 2. Tool 69: Radar Chart is good for this.
5 Complete the diagram on the page opposite, considering carefully what each of the groups of stakeholders would need to experience to believe the brand you are aiming for. For example, questions like: 'As a customer what would prove to me that the company is . . . ?'

6 Create an action plan to move the brand towards the desired brand image. (This may require further exploration into what would change the brand image in this area for these people.) Questions to aid the development of an action plan: 'Who and what is it that projects the brand of the business?' 'Who needs to be responsible for changing it?' 'Is it feasible to move the brand or would it be more beneficial to start up a new business branded differently?' 'Is the brand in line with the business strategy?'

■ Example
For a chocolate bar.

■ Exercise
Develop a brand development strategy for a new high-quality airline.

■ Key points
Brand is made up of a number of different elements and is tied intrinsically to the individual or group perception.

The brand image you are aiming for will affect where you advertise, market and sell the product or service. It will also impact how you price and package it. The brand needs to be readily identifiable, e.g. Rolls-Royce, Microsoft, or Virgin.

You can use more than four groups of stakeholders for a more focused approach.

■ Additional comments
Building a brand is often harder than destroying it. Take for example the leader of a health company; all it would take would be one cigarette to undermine the brand.

Branding issues often follow acquisitions, i.e. should we rebrand the acquired company's products or services or should we continue to use its name. Using a large number of trading names within a group will weaken the branding.

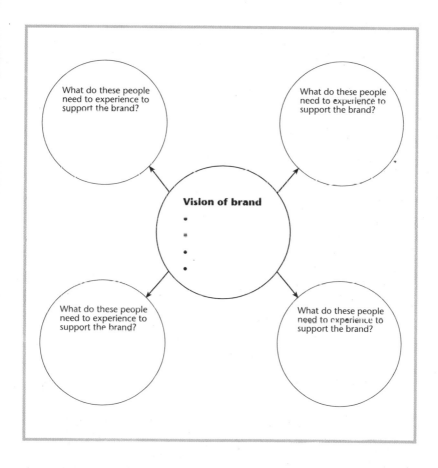

6

Breakeven Analysis

When to use
As a short-term planning tool in conjunction with other financial and non-financial analysis.

What you get
A prediction of the number or value of sales required to recoup the costs and begin to make a profit.

Time
With all of the data available the construction of the graph should take no more than half-an-hour.

Number of people
One to construct the chart.

Equipment
Computer spreadsheet or graph paper and pen.

Method
1   Identify the fixed costs: those costs which, in the short term, remain unchanged within a relevant range of activity (time frame, normally about 5 years), e.g. rent of buildings, equipment.
2   Identify the variable costs that in the short term vary with output, within the same range (time frame) as above, e.g. materials, transportation.
3   Identify the predicted output in units over the range (time frame), e.g. Year One – 200 widgets.
4   Identify the sales value for the range (time frame). In Year One, 1 widget provides £3 revenue.
5   Draw up a graph with money (cost and value) on the vertical axis, and units on the horizontal axis.
6   Insert the sales line, the fixed-costs line (which runs parallel to the base of the chart), insert the total-costs line, which is the fixed costs plus the variable costs.
7   Where the total-costs line crosses with the sales line is the breakeven point.

Example
Output – 125,000 units
Sales – £500,000
Variable costs – £250,000
Fixed costs – £100,000
From the diagram we can see that the breakeven point is at 40,000 units of production.

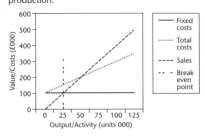

Exercise
Complete a breakeven analysis for the following facts:
Output – £220,000
Sales – £440,000
Variable costs – £160,000
Fixed costs – £20,000

Key points
All costs in the long term are variable.
   Breakeven quantity can also be calculated by:

Breakeven quantity = Fixed costs/(Sales – Variable costs)

The breakeven quantity provides you with the point at which profits for that project are zero.

Additional comments
Breakeven analysis provides a very linear analysis of a project. It is useful to provide comparative breakeven analysis on project options. Still the measure is purely financial so it is important to consider other aspects of the project in terms of benefits and downsides.
   The quality of the output is fundamentally dependent on the quality of information that is put into the analysis.
   The fixed costs will include all overheads, capital equipment and establishment costs. The costs that are incurred even if no products are made.

The variable costs are those directly associated with producing the product: material costs, labour costs and consumable costs and are normally expressed as a cost per unit.

■ **Other information**
There are lots of books that cover this area including: E. Brigham and J. Houston, *Fundamentals of Financial Management*, Harcourt Brace College Publishers, 2000; A. Hawkins, *The Managing Cash Flow Pocket Book*, Management Pocket Books, 1995.

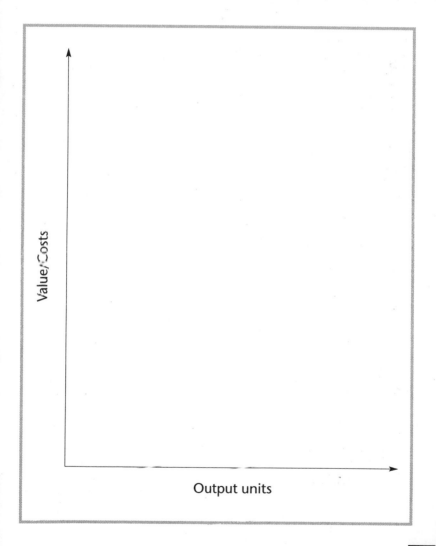

7

Business Design and Improvement

▨ When to use
When considering carrying out business design or an improvement project in any part of the business.

▨ What you get
A holistic approach to business system design.

▨ Time
Depends on the size, scale and scope of the project. An overview of the elements it will need to contain will take about 1 day.

▨ Number of people
A multifunctional team of people will need to head up the project. Involvement from all stakeholders will be important throughout the project. The core team needs to be full time.

▨ Equipment
A clearly visible plan and review mechanism – see Tools 36: Gantt Chart; 71: Road Mapping and 2: Balanced Scorecard.

▨ Method
1 Identify objectives, e.g. quality, market share, level of inventory, cost reduction and duration of the project.
2 Create project team – ensure both suitability and capability of team are considered (right skills, right mix and right attitude). See Tools 77: Skills Matrix; 86: Team Working and 75: Shared Values.
3 Analyse the existing way of working and environment. Useful tools: 83: SWOT Analysis; 89: Time Based Process Mapping; 57: Order Qualifiers and Order Winners; 31: Flowcharting; 27: External Analysis (PEST).
4 Design the new. Give an overview of the basic subsystems and objectives (top-down approach) and develop a detailed design by empowered employees (bottom-up approach). Integrating the two approaches provides a holistic approach. Initially design from a logical perspective, then consider how it will cope when working (steady-state and dynamic design).
5 Develop suitable controls for the design, ensuring the controls are useful, simple and don't cause any unwanted knock-on effects. Tool 78: Solution Effect Analysis is useful for checking this.
6 Implement the design. Plan this stage carefully; it is important that the implementation does not have a detrimental impact on the customer. Consider communication, training requirements, problem identification, resource requirements etc.
7 Monitor and improve – use suitable measures to monitor and reward improvements. Enrol all stakeholders in the continuous improvement. See Tool 40: Improvement Cycle.

▨ Example
A project may be to improve the hospitality services for a company. This would require a team of people from across the organisation. There would need to be some focused objectives, an understanding of the current situation, a new way of working would need to be designed, suitable controls agreed and then reviews put in place to continuously improve.

▨ Exercise
Use the approach to design a fitness programme.

▨ Key points
This tool provides a holistic framework for business design, it is important that it is moulded to your organisation's needs. It is important to keep the design as simple as possible. A successful design is useless if people don't buy into the new way of working. Total commitment is required from senior management to make it work.

Effectiveness comes before efficiency – make sure you are doing the right job before you worry about how well you are doing it.

▨ Additional comments
It is an iterative process: don't expect a 'right answer'.

There are many processes and models to aid business design, this is just one which is simple and yet flexible enough to work in many situations.

■ Other information

Further information can be found in
M. Hammer and J. Champy, *Reengineering the
Corporation*, Nicholas Brealey, 1993 and
L. Miller, *Business Process Re-engineering: A
Management Guidebook* (2nd ed), Vertical
Systems, Inc., 1996.

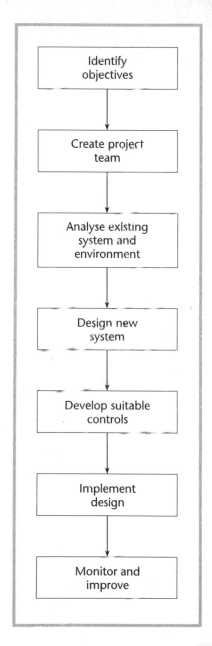

8

Business Ethics

When to use
Whenever you are doing business.

What you get
A simple set of rules, which will advise all who work for you what is expected of them when they do business.

Time
3–4 hours to get a group of people to understand the issues faced by the people in your company when doing business.

Number of people
5–15 from across the organisation. It is fundamentally important that senior management are represented.

Equipment
The checklist shown on the page opposite and a flipchart or wipe board to capture the output from the session.

Method
1 Go through each of the items on the checklist, and consider for each one, what would be appropriate behaviour for the company. This will provide the backbone of the 'ethics code'.
2 Develop an action plan to support the elements that are highlighted in the step above.
3 Develop an effective (appropriate for your company and your employees) method of disseminating the output (ethics code) across your organisation. Think also about how you 'police' it. What happens if the code is broken?

Example

Areas for consideration	Suggested guidelines
Purchasing	Gifts of an advertising nature of modest value can be accepted. Offers of entertainment can only be accepted if part of a group and can be reciprocated. Gifts of cash cannot be accepted. All acceptances to be declared to supervisor.
Selling	Gifts of an advertising nature of modest value can be offered, dinner meetings and modest group entertainment can be offered. Gifts of cash in any form cannot be offered. All must be formally recorded.
Purchasing internationally	Operate within the law of the selling and purchasing companies' national laws. This brings UK buyers into line with purchasing in the UK, i.e. no financial incentive to be accepted.
Selling internationally	Operate within the law of both the purchasing and selling country, therefore, no direct incentive should be offered. However, if it is normal in the purchasing country to trade through in-country agents, the agents themselves may wish to offer a sales incentive. This must never be priced into the contract, nor should any element of the discount or commission offered to the agent be earmarked for such purposes. Agents' commission must be modest and commensurate with the work carried out.
Competition	Do not make adverse comments about competitor's products or services. All comparisons need to be factual.
Bidding and negotiations	All bids should be made based on information provided and knowledge obtained by legal means. All negotiations are to be conducted with integrity; you should never try to outsmart the buyer or seller.

■ Exercise

Negotiate with a child how much pocket money he or she should have. Consider how you would do this without resorting to some form of bribery, dishonesty, or attempting to outsmart your child.

■ Key points

You must get the group to discuss each item fully and agree what is expected of people.

A code of ethics is important as without one, people make their own assessment of what is expected of them, which may be very different to what the company expects.

The checklist prepared is not complete as many businesses, whether manufacturing or service face a whole host of areas where business ethics can have a profound impact on the success of the company such as:

- environment
- recruitment and motivation of people
- financial incentives to employees
- share ownership
- relationships with stockmarket and bankers
- relationship with regulators

■ Additional comments

People can occasionally see the development and integration of business ethics as being over constraining to individuals, or just common sense. Business ethics must not be seen as a behavioural conformity procedure. It is about being open and clear about expectations.

■ Other information

Further information can be found: G. Chryssides and J Kaler, *An Introduction to Business Ethics*, Thomson Business Press, 1993.

Areas for consideration	Issues to consider	Suggested guidelines
Purchasing	Gifts or offers of entertainment to buyers from selling companies.	
Selling	Gifts or offers of entertainment to customers.	
Purchasing internationally	Is the law of selling country different to UK, i.e. is interest legal, does the law of the selling country allow financial sales incentives?	
Selling internationally	Is the law of the purchasing country different to UK, I.e. is a financial incentive for a contract legal?	
Competition	Do not make adverse comments about competitor's products or services. All comparisons need to be factual.	
Bidding and negotiations	Soliciting information about competitors or bids that is not generally available. Lack of integrity during negotiation.	

9

Business Excellence Framework

When to use

When needing to understand the bigger picture for achieving business excellence. Particularly useful as a communication tool.

What you get

A framework to work around to enable a holistic approach to business excellence.

Time

To develop and implement all of the issues surrounding the framework will take about 12 months.

Number of people

The whole organisation.

Equipment

Visible displays of progress.

Method

1 Develop a 'vision' for the organisation. See Tool 91: Visioning – The Future. The 'vision' is a statement of 'what you want to be'. It needs to be simple, clear, meaningful and written in the present tense.

2 Determine the company's values and beliefs. See Tool 75: Shared Values to help here. This provides an understanding of 'who you want to be'. It is important that all employees buy into the values.

3 Develop the business strategy to support the achievement of the vision. See the Project Matrix at the front of the book for useful tools.

4 Develop a clear mission, which needs to contain the purpose and scope of the organisation, i.e. 'what do we do'. It is fundamentally important that people are brought into the vision, values and mission, and understand their role in making it happen.

5 Develop the critical success factors (CSFs), this is about creating a picture of what success will look like. See Tool 2: Balanced Scorecard for a balanced approach to this. Develop and put in place key performance indicators (KPIs) to monitor progress and clearly understood targets to aim at.

6 Develop the core processes to enable the achievement of the mission. An approach to help is Tool 7: Business Design and Improvement.

7 Manage the processes to continuously improve and get closer and closer to the vision.

Example

Vision	The UK's best railway company
Values	Clean, safe, trains on time, at times when customer requires them with genuinely caring employees offering a standard of service beyond expectations. Company and employee integrity to be recognised by passengers on our trains.
Mission	Frequent services on secondary line between non-intercity stations in Midlands and London using modern rolling stock.
CSFs	Trained empowered staff rewarded on success of operation New rolling stock On-time service to customer-required timescales Low Cost Happy employees
KPIs	Customer care surveys Passenger load factors Age of rolling stock Profitability
Core processes	Identification of customer needs Training of employees Train scheduling and management

Exercise

Consider all of the elements for your own company. Are there any contradictions or missing links?

▪ Key points

The communication and involvement of all employees throughout the process is key. It is from the core processes downward (on the diagram below) that the vision is delivered; ensure the project momentum continues well into that area. It is the hard bit and will require everyone working together to make it happen.

You need to make the process yours. It is useful to say the framework has worked elsewhere, but you need to give it your organisation's identity.

Don't be afraid to get external help, it is much cheaper to learn from other people's mistakes!

▪ Additional comments

Don't expect miracles. Miracles do happen but you have to work hard at them.

▪ Other information

For further information on business excellence, see British Quality Foundation – www.quality-foundation.co.uk or European Centre for Business Excellence, www.ecforbe.com also EFQM – European Foundation for Quality Management.

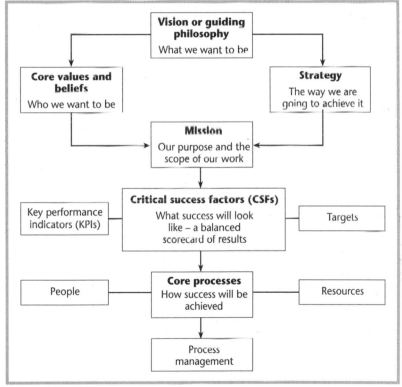

Source: Oakland Consulting plc. Reprinted with kind permission; John S. Oakland, *Total Organizational Excellence*, page 8, Figure 2.1, Butterworth-Heinemann, 1999.

Cause and Effect Analysis

When to use
When a problem has many elements, and it is necessary to identify the root cause of a problem as distinct from the symptoms.

What you get
It develops a holistic and logical representation of a problem broken down into a pictorial format.

Time
From half-an-hour to 4 hours depending on level of detail required.

Number of people
For best results 2–10 people.

Equipment
A large area visible to all, which can be written on.

> It is better to have too much space than not enough.

Method
1 Identify the problem or effect to be addressed and write it on the right of the diagram.
2 Determine the major areas that contribute to the effect and put them on the end of the bones.
3 Collect the causes within each of the major areas that contribute to the effect.

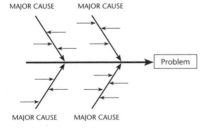

4
Ask 'why' of the causes to get to the root cause.
5 Collect data to understand the impact of these causes on the overall problem, see Tool 92: Vital Few Analysis.
6 Prioritise the causes to improve for maximum benefit, see Tool 26: Effort Impact Graph.

Example

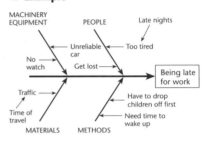

Exercise
Build a cause and effect diagram for the problem of not having enough hours in the day.

Key points
It is important to ask 'why', this is what breaks the symptoms back to their root causes. Common major areas are: plant, equipment, materials, people, environment and methods. If ideas are slow coming use these to prompt, e.g. 'What in people is causing . . .?' 'They were so busy fighting off the alligators, no one had time to consider draining the swamp'.

Additional comments
These are sometimes called 'Fishbone' or 'Ishikawa' diagrams.
These sessions can also be run in reverse. That is, the group brainstorms a whole host of causes of a problem. These 'brainstormed' causes can then be grouped into Major Causes on a diagram. Sometimes this approach helps people to see interactions between causes and appreciate other people's issues.

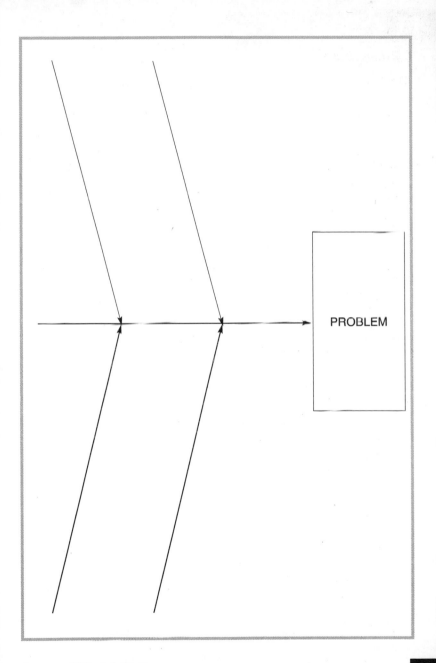

11

Change Cycle

When to use
To prepare for and to help manage through any change.

What you get
A means of explaining, understanding and securing buy-in to the process of change.

Time
Half-an-hour to explain the model, 2 hours to develop ideas with a small group.

Number of people
It can be useful to explain the model to everyone involved in a project. After the explanation, smaller groups of approximately six can brainstorm action plans.

Equipment
Copies of the model and the template opposite for all people in the team.

Method
1 Explain that the model is being used to help work through the change that you are currently involved in or are proposing.
2 Explain how the model works and the four stages that people pass through during a change (see the example).
3 Use an example of a change that most people can relate to and discuss with the team how the model describes this change. You could use your own example from the following exercise.
4 Get the team to discuss and brainstorm the types of behaviour that they would expect to see during each of the four stages in relation to the current project. (For larger teams, split into smaller groups of approximately six.)
5 Review the behaviours and record them using the template opposite.
6 Get the team to discuss and brainstorm suitable actions to address the behaviours they identify. These actions should try to help people move forward towards the next stage of the model and acceptance of the change. (For larger teams split into smaller groups.)

7 Based on the list of ideas, agree on an action plan to help people work through and accept the current change.

Example
The first stage is denial – *that's a good idea, but it won't work here*. This is followed by irritation or anger – *look, we told you it wouldn't work*. During the third stage people start to explore the idea – *maybe there's something to this*. The final stage is commitment to the new idea – *I always knew that this would work*.

Exercise
Use the model and template to think about moving house.

Key points
Effectiveness tends to suffer while people work through the stages before committing to the new idea. Ideally, you want people to get to the commitment stage as quickly as possible. It is worth considering that different people may be at different stages in the cycle.

Getting the group to work through the model is the first stage in achieving buy-in and commitment.

Be cautious if things seem to be going well. During the more difficult stages people's behaviour tends to be hidden.

Early in the project, people will tend to look backwards to the security of what they already know. Change and the future can be unsettling for some people.

■ Additional comments

If anyone is cynical about the model, don't worry; they are just working through the first two stages. Many projects are greeted with initial enthusiasm – *about time something got done*. This tends to disappear when people realise that they will also have to change.

The four stages are similar to what happens with a new team. First it *forms*, then it *storms* (arguments), hopefully it then *reforms* so that it can start to *perform*.

■ Other information

Based on concepts from E. Kubler Ross, *On Death and Dying*, Collier Books, 1983.

	Looking to the past	Looking to the future	
Confidence, morale and effectiveness	**Stage 1.** Denial Behaviours and Indicators Actions/Solutions	**Stage 4.** Commitment Behaviours and Indicators Actions/Solutions	Open behaviour
	Stage 2. Irritation Behaviours and Indicators Actions/Solutions	**Stage 3.** Exploring Behaviours and Indicators Actions/Solutions	Hidden behaviour

Time

12

Climate for Change Indicator

▓ When to use
As part of a change programme. Before, during and after the change programme as a way to monitor, develop and improve.

▓ What you get
A pictorial indication of where people or groups of people in your organisation are in terms of five key success factors for change. Provides an indication of areas that require attention.

▓ Time
Time taken to do the research will depend on the sample size; ideally if it were done as part of a workshop the collection of information would take about 1 hour. The analysis and actions required normally take substantially longer.

▓ Number of people
Ideally everyone who is involved in the change programme should be asked for his or her input. Understanding that often this is not feasible, a fair and broad selection of people should be involved.

▓ Equipment
The maturity matrix* on pages 26–7.

▓ Method
1. Determine the ideal levels for each of the key success factors for change. Use the maturity opposite to score the ideal ratings. The following table gives you a little more information on each one.
2. Determine the sample to be analysed.
3. Carry out the analysis by providing people with a copy of the maturity matrix and get them to score each of the factors for their organisation, with respect to the change programme.
4. Collect all of the completed sheets and plot the average scores for the sample on a radar chart, see Tool 69: Radar Chart. Also put on the chart the ideal positions for each of the factors that were determined in step 1.

Commitment	The recognition that change is an integral part of the business strategy. Includes senior level commitment, time, resources, etc.
People – social and cultural	Mainly concerned with the 'people' element of change. Includes behaviour, perceptions, attitude, etc.
Communication	Both internal and external communication. Includes timing, methods, content, etc.
Methods – tools	Project management methodologies, knowledge and skills to implement the change.
Interactions	Methods to deal with interactions within the organisation. Including managing the balance between normal operations and other changes in the organisation.

5. Analyse the findings and identify actions that would help to move the 'real' line to the 'ideal' line. Present findings back to all concerned. Carry out the actions.
6. Run the process again to monitor and continuously improve.

▓ Example
The key actions indicated by the chart below are that training and development in appropriate methods need to be carried out in the company.

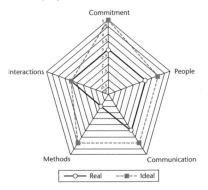

Climate for Change Indicator

▦ Exercise

Run through the exercise filling in the chart for you in your organisation.

▦ Key points

Rather than using your own predetermined 'ideal' case for each of the factors, it is possible to identify best practice and use it as a benchmarking tool.

It is important that a balanced approach between the key success factors is taken. Focusing purely in one area will have detrimental affects on the others.

The tool can be used at many levels from strategic decision making to small project management.

It is possible to add another factor into the maturity matrix if there is another area that is specifically fundamental to your company.

▦ Other information

*Dr A. Clarke, Engineering Doctorate, Improving the Change Management Process, Executive Summary, 1996. See also A. Clarke and J. Garside, The development of a best practice model for change management, *European Management Journal*, Vol. 15, No. 5, 537–545, 1997.

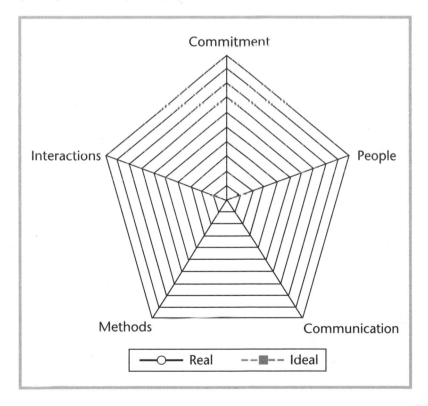

Maturity matrix

Level	Commitment	People	Communication	Methods	Interactions
5	**Full and visible commitment**: visible commitment from top and throughout the company at all stages of project – including post-implementation, everyone in the organisation buys-in to the change.	**Culture which is fully committed to change**: those affected by change are involved from start to finish, change seen as vital to the business; people issues are addressed throughout the project; impact of the change on individuals fully addressed; team works well together and team spirit is excellent.	**Excellent communication**: everyone in organisation (including customers and suppliers) understands need for change, what is being done throughout the change, throughout the implementation and the impact the change will have on the business.	**Always used**: project management is used well and consistently throughout; everyone in team understands need and can use it; multidisciplinary co-located project team with full-time project manager; training identified and given before project starts and throughout the project.	**Excellent management of interactions**: change is part of the business plan; senior person in the business full time on change management; good balance of long- and short-term change projects; good balance of operations work and change projects; resource management good.
4	**Good commitment but inconsistent or absent at times**: clear direction from steering committee; clear ownership of tasks; all those impacted by the change are involved right from the start and throughout the project; virtually everyone across company buys-in to the change.	**Culture which readily accepts change**: most of those affected from start and are involved from throughout; most people consider the change worthwhile; people issues are usually addressed; impact of the change on individuals widely understood; team works well most of the time and team spirit is good.	**Very good communication**: most people in the organisation at all levels understand the need for the change, what the changes are and how it will impact on the business.	**Usually used**: project management is used consistently throughout; many people in team understand and can use it; benchmarking usually done; project team is multidisciplinary; often co-located with full-time project manager; training identified and given at start of project.	**Very good management of interactions**: changes are mostly in business plan; senior person with responsibility for change management; good balance of operations and change projects; little consideration to long- and short-term balance; occasional problems with resource management an issue.
3	**Some visible commitment – often consistent but low level**: full-time project manager, project owner at senior level; many of people in project team own the change; few resource constraints; all	**Culture which accepts change**: many of those affected by change are involved from start and throughout; change is regarded as important to business but inconvenient; impact of the change on individuals discussed;	**Good communication**: all project team, most senior managers and many people throughout the company understand the need for the change, what the changes are and how it will impact on the business.	**Often used**: most aspects of project management are used; one or two people in team can use it; multidisciplinary project team with project manager; training identified and given at start of project.	**Good management of interactions**: changes are often part of the business plan but some unplanned; senior person in the business full time on change management; operational work v. change projects conflicts;

	Commitment	Culture	Communication	Project management	Management of interactions
	members of team attend meetings, operational v. project conflicts at times; most people buy-in to the change.	team works well but lacks team spirit; at times people issues are sometimes included.			resource management sometimes an issue.
2	**Limited & inconsistent commitment:** no steering committee; project owner not interested or not senior enough; sporadic attendance at project meetings; operations take priority over projects tasks; limited buy-in across company; few people completely buy-in to project.	**Culture which reluctantly accepts change:** few of those affected by change are involved from start and throughout; change seen as necessary evil; few people understand implications of the change on them; limited teamwork with no real team spirit.	**Limited communication:** most of project team, and some managers understand the need for the change, what the changes are and how it will impact on the business.	**Sometimes used:** some aspects of project management are used; at least one person in team uses it; multidisciplinary project team with project manager; little training carried out.	**Limited management of interactions:** changes are often planned but seldom formalised; senior person with responsibility for change management; operational work takes priority; resource problems often arise.
1	**Poor commitment:** project team members often pulled off to operational duties; only select few people buy-in to the change; few team members regularly attend meetings; resources (people and equipment) are a problem.	**Culture which is very wary of change:** virtually no one affected by change is involved throughout; few people believe the change is worth doing; the impact of the change on individuals has not been addressed; no real teamwork or spirit.	**Poor communication:** some managers understand the need for the change, what the changes are and how it will impact on the business but only project team knows progress being made.	**Seldom used:** only one or two aspects of project management used at certain times in the project; no one really knows how to use all of it; team approach used; no training given specifically to team before or during project.	**Poor management of interactions:** most changes are unplanned; no one responsible for change management (shared); good balance of operations and change projects operations have to take priority, changes are usually under-resourced.
0	**No commitment:** little top level support; poorly attended project team meetings; people involved in change only when operational duties are slacker; no support or buy-in across the company.	**Culture which does not readily accept change:** change considered waste of time; no one in organisation knows or has considered the implications of the project on them; few believe that the change is worth doing; no teamwork.	**No communication:** hardly anyone knows the importance of the project, what is going on and how it can influence the business.	**Never used:** project management never used; benchmarking never used no real project teams; no training given to people involved in implementing change.	**No management of interactions:** changes are always unplanned, under-resourced and always take second place to operations; no one responsible for managing change.

Communication

When to use

When needing to improve communication, or as a warm up to an improving communications session.

What you get

An awareness of the elements needed for good communication.

Time

30 minutes to 1 hour will provide a substantial insight.

Number of people

Groups of about 10 are ideal, larger groups can split into smaller ones but the exercise must be run in different rooms. Smaller groups work but it is important that the key elements of successful communication are not decided by a small group and enforced on the rest of the organisation, as the benefits will be significantly reduced.

Equipment

The diagrams shown opposite and paper and pens for the entire group.

Method

1 A volunteer is given a copy of the diagram at the top of the opposite page, be clear that they cannot show the diagram to anyone else. Facing away from the rest of the group, with no questions and no feedback allowed, ask them to describe the diagram for the rest of the group to draw. The rest of the group can talk to each other.

2 When completed, look at all of the pictures from the group. Notice the differences and the similarities.

3 Lead a discussion on what helps communication. Note down the key elements.

4 Run the exercise again with the other diagram, putting into practice the key elements for successful communication and analyse the results.

5 Relate the key elements for successful communication back to the workplace. Would they hold true there? What can we do to improve communication there?

Example

After the first two steps, the group all have very different pictures, the orientation of the paper is different, the connections are different, etc.

Key elements for successful communication:

- feedback
- questions
- visual aids
- clear boundaries
- clear assumptions
- keep it simple
- don't make assumptions about what people know.

Running the exercise again, using the elements identified for good communication, most of the diagrams were the same.

Exercise

Run the exercise with a close friend or one of your family.

Key points

Although a very simplistic exercise, it quickly highlights areas where communication can immediately be improved in everyday business.

Additional comments

The simplistic nature of the tool means that some elements of everyday life are not included:

- It is rare that we have the full picture.
- It assumes that everyone needs to know the information.
- Methods and means of communication, it is rare that all of the people who need the information are all sat in the same room.

To increase the usefulness of the tool, consider the elements that stop successful communication in the business, and work solutions to those as well.

14

Competitive Product Placement

■ When to use
When analysing a product range as part of a strategy review.

■ What you get
A pictorial representation of products or groups of products positioning in terms of relative competitive position, market growth rate and an assessment of position in the product life cycle.

■ Time
1–2 hours will provide a useful discussion.

■ Number of people
3–8 people, preferably from different parts of the business. It is important that there is a representation from sales and/or marketing.

■ Equipment
Flipchart or wipe board to create the matrix and somewhere to capture useful discussion points.

■ Method
1 Draw up the matrix shown opposite and agree the scales for each of the axes. It is important that the scales are appropriate for your business.
2 Place your products or groups of products on the matrix fixing their position in terms of relative market share and market growth rate.
3 Discuss the implications of the product positioning.
   Dogs: Low market share, low market growth – Do we want to continue producing this? Why? What would happen if we stopped this product line? How can we maximise its usefulness?
   Cash cows: High market share, low market growth – How long will it maintain cash cow status? Are there any options to increase the market growth?

Question marks: Low market share, high market growth – Is there anything we can do to increase market share? What movements in market share are happening in the marketplace?
Stars: High market share, high market growth – Have we got any stars? Where are we going to get a constant source of stars from? How long will they stay stars?
4 Consider the balance of the portfolio. The absence of stars may lead to no cash cows in the future, no cash cows now may lead to cash flow problems. Too many question marks may drain the business of cash if ambitious levels of market share are aimed at.
5 Use this perspective of the business to aid strategy development.

■ Example

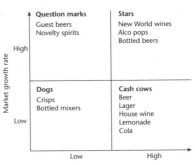

Relative market share

■ Exercise
Complete the matrix for a theme park.

■ Key points
This is a useful tool for understanding an organisation's situation or market position and as a basis for internal managerial debate.

The questions in step 3 of the method are a sample of the types of discussion points that can be raised.

It isn't always possible or necessary to get accurate information on positioning on the grid; simply using the high, low relative measures still provides a useful discussion.

This tool can be used for service offerings as well as products.

▓ Additional comments

Due to the tool's simplistic nature it often fails to represent the complexities of markets. Therefore do not use in isolation. Growth and market share are not the only factors that make markets attractive.

▓ Other information

Diagram adapted and reprinted from *Long Range Planning 10*, B. Hadley, 'Strategy and the Business Portfolio', p. 12, Copyright (February, 1977), with permission from Excerpta Medica Inc.

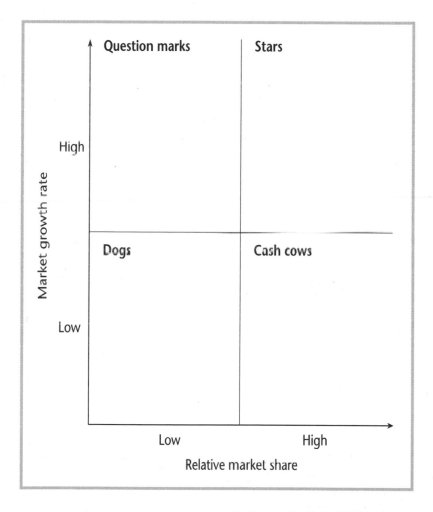

Reprinted from *Long Range Planning, 10*, B. Hadley, 'Strategy and the Business Portfolio', p. 12, Copyright (February, 1977), with permission from Excerpta Medica Inc.

15

Competitor Analysis

When to use
As part of a strategy review.

What you get
An insight into the industry and markets in which you compete. An understanding of the important issues to address in your strategy.

Time
A half-day workshop will provide useful insight. More time is needed for an in-depth review.

Number of people
A group of about six from various parts of the company usually works best.

Equipment
Background data relating to your business in terms of suppliers, customers, substitutes, new entrants and competitors.

Method
1 Work through each of the elements in turn.
2 *Suppliers* – Who are they? How many of them are there? Do they deal with our competitors? How significant is our business to them? Are there alternative suppliers?
3 *Buyers* – Ask similar questions to those for suppliers.
4 *Substitutes* – What products might remove demand for ours? What new technologies might make our products redundant? (e.g. IT might reduce the need for business class air travel).
5 *Potential entrants* – What barriers prevent entering or leaving our market – start-up costs, distribution infrastructure, brand image, etc? What factors attract new entrants – high profits, new market, regulation, etc?
6 *Competitors* – Who are they? What are their strengths and weaknesses? How will they respond to what we do?
7 Capture the results of these discussions.
8 Prioritise the issues and develop actions to address them (for tools to help see Project Matrix or Day-to-Day Matrix).

Example
The following example is based on a consumer electronics company. It specialises in analysing existing products, copying the technology, then selling cut-down basic versions at very competitive prices.

1 *Suppliers* – Reliant on a few key outside contractors who also supply our larger major competitors. There is currently a slight lack of capacity in the supply base.

> *Partnership maybe?*

2 *Buyers* – Have recently taken over our distributors. Existing programmes are developing relationships with retail outlets and reviewing our IT systems for ordering and scheduling.
3 *Substitutes* – The industry expects to have new technologies appearing on a fairly regular basis. Our strategy is to follow the technology and repackage it as a cheaper alternative to the premier brands. Our consumers are spending more on outdoor pursuits.
4 *Potential entrants* – We are repackaging other people's technology and have managed to grow very rapidly. There is little to stop others copying our idea or premier companies re-releasing older products under a different brand name.

> *An attractive market and low barrier to entry – trouble!*

5 *Competitors* – We have no direct competition at the cheap end of the market. However, our rapid growth has attracted attention and some premier brands are beginning to release products in our segment.

Exercise
Complete a competitor analysis for your local supermarket. Are they in a competitive position?

▓ Key points
You need to understand your position in the industry and exploit opportunities while covering your weaknesses. In most markets, profitability is self-balancing being determined by the risks from the barriers to entry against the barriers to exit. Highly profitable markets attract 'niche' entrants.

▓ Additional comments
You might group suppliers and/or customers into major types to simplify the process.

Typical solutions to issues raised during the exercise include partnership, acquisition, investigating new markets, erecting barriers to entry by using patents or advertising the brand.

▓ Other information
Concept developed by Michael Porter, *Competitive Advantage of Nations*, Macmillan, 1998, reproduced with permission of Palgrave.

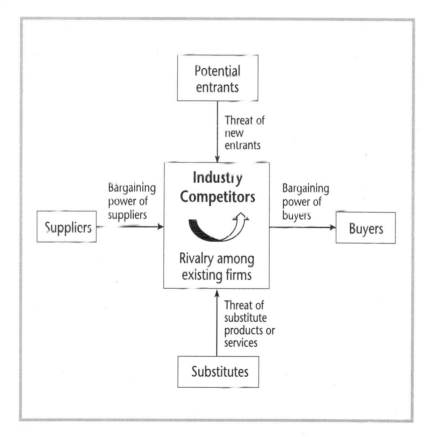

Source: Michael Porter, *Competitive Advantage of Nations*, Macmillan, 1998, reproduced with permission of Palgrave.

16

Concept Fan

When to use
When a brainstorming group needs more help and structure or where you want a group to see the bigger picture.

What you get
This tool produces lots of creative solutions in a logical manner. It also helps to identify the major issues and increase understanding of a problem.

Time
Time will vary depending on the scale of the problem. Typically half-an-hour to 1 hour sessions produce good results.

Number of people
Can be used individually or with large groups. Typically a group of four to six is ideal.

Equipment
A large wipe board is ideal. Large sheets of paper with space to lay them out can also work.

Method
1 Write down the problem or the desired outcome in simple (ideally one-word) terms.
2 Ask the question 'why' is this a problem. Write down any answers in simple terms to the right of the original statement.
3 Ask the question 'how' can we solve this problem. Write down any answers in simple terms to the left of the original statement.

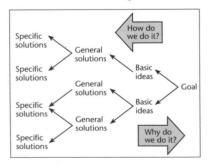

4 Repeat this process for every statement that is written down until the group runs out of ideas.
5 Rewrite the final fan neatly and give copies to all participants. The reasons for tackling the problem will be shown on the right of the fan while ideas and solutions will appear on the left.

Example
The concept fan opposite is an example of what might be produced if the technique was used to generate ideas for a company's quality improvement programme.

Exercise
Complete a concept fan for the problem of cooking an egg.

Key points
In practice, the chart is complete when one side shows the fundamental issue being addressed while the other side lists specific actions relating to this issue. For example, if a concept fan was being completed for a business quality programme, one side might state the overall issue as 'improving business performance through quality'. The other side would list specific actions such as improving operator training or implementing statistical process control techniques.

Additional comments
The concept fan is limited by people's willingness and ability to get involved – use an icebreaker at the start of the session.

To help get things started, the facilitator can fill in part of the fan to show how it works.

Sometimes it is not necessary to start by writing down the overall objective. It is often useful to jump in with a current issue and then keep asking 'why' in order to work back to the main objective. This helps develop awareness of the 'bigger picture'.

Unfortunately the fan does not provide an answer as to which of the solutions is best. However, in simple terms, any solution that has a high number of connections (particularly leading to the right of the chart) is likely to be influential.

A good book on creativity is: Edward De Bono,
*Serious Creativity – Using the Power of Lateral
Thinking to Create New Ideas,* HarperCollins
Business, 1996. See Tools 26: Effort Impact
Graph and 23: Decision Tables for help on
choosing from the list of ideas created.

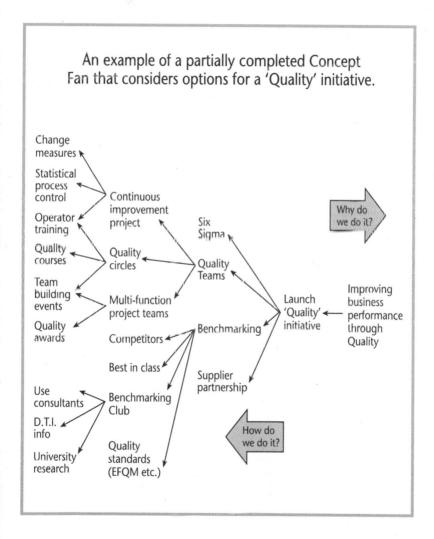

An example of a partially completed Concept Fan that considers options for a 'Quality' initiative.

17

Creating a Financial Business Case

■ When to use
To provide a financial business case to justify the investment in a project, equipment or business.

■ What you get
A business case, which sets the cost of the investment against the projected return over a period of time, together with an assessment of the financial return from different business scenarios.

■ Time
From 2–4 hours for a small project to days for a larger multifaceted business or project.

■ Number of people
1–2 people.

■ Equipment
The business case can be prepared using an accounts analysis pad but it is much more effective when produced on a computer spreadsheet.

■ Method
1 Fully understand the costs associated with the project particularly the phasing of the cash flow, i.e. the points at which cash will flow out of the company over the life of the project. Do not forget any additional overhead costs, e.g. people, tooling, design and possible trials. Also build in a contingency to recover from any shortcomings.

2 Fully understand all the elements of the project that have come together to make the project whole and the costs and cash flow at each stage. See Tool 94: Work Package Breakdown.

3 Set up the analysis chart or spreadsheet with the vertical axis showing all items of expenditure and when the cash flow is expected to occur on the horizontal axis.

4 Also set up on the analysis sheet or spreadsheet all of the items where cost is saved or revenue generated on the vertical axis and when the benefits are expected to

be achieved on the horizontal axis. From this it is possible to generate a graph of costs outflow and inflow to determine the cash payback period.

5 From the above, it is possible to calculate the return on investment over any period of time. Initially the return on investment will be negative until the cash flow breakeven point is reached.

6 It is now necessary to calculate the value of the investment at today's date. There are a number of financial methods available to do this. The one detailed here is the discounted cash flow (DCF) which discounts the return on the investment in the later years for the expected currency inflation and cost of borrowing. The DCF is calculated by putting an interest cost on the capital used to breakeven point and reducing the return value by inflation back to today's date.

7 It is now necessary to understand how sensitive your business case is likely to be to changes in the market environment, possible delays in introduction of the project and maybe changes in the cost of borrowing or inflation. Look specifically at its impact on cash flow and the business. This can be done easily using a spreadsheet.

■ Example
See page opposite.

■ Exercise
Consider investing in an energy efficient light bulb, taking the claims of the electricity savings made by the manufacturer, the lost opportunity of the investment at your current bank interest rate, the manufacturer's life of the bulb compared to a normal light bulb etc.

■ Key points
This financial evaluation of a project provides one element of a justification; it does not take into account the positive or negative impact on the less tangible issues, like branding, quality or market positioning in terms of achieving the company's strategic goals. Tools to help link measures, both financial and non-financial to strategy are, Tools 2: Balanced Scorecard or 35: Forward Measurement.

Other information

There are many financial books in the market, here are a few to get you started: E. F. Brigham, *Fundamentals of Financial Management*, Holt-Saunders International Editions, 1983; J. Covello and B. Hazelgren, *Your First Business Plan: A Simple Question and Answer Format Designed to Help you Write your Own Plan*, Source Books, 1997; B. Finch, *30 Minutes to Write a Business Plan*, Kogan Page, 1997.

Cash flow analysis (Simple)

This simple version does not take into account the lost opportunity of interest earned on the outstanding cash balance. It suggests the breakeven point would be Year 4.

	Year	1	2	3	4	5	6
£k	Expenditure	100	0	0	0	0	0
£k	Savings	25	25	25	25	25	25
£k	Cash flow	(75)	25	25	25	25	25
£k	Cumulative cash flow @ year end	(75)	(50)	(25)	0	25	25

However, a company could expect to earn say 10 per cent on the capital invested. Note that when this is included now the breakeven point is between Years 5 and 6.

	Year	1	2	3	4	5	6
£k	Lost interest opportunity	10	8.5	6.9	5.04	3.04	0.84
£k	Balance to be recovered	85	68.5	50.4	30.9	8.4	(15.7)

Net present value (NPV)

The basic idea for NPV is to value the benefits of the investment in today's money, i.e. the date the investment was made. To do this you will be required to understand what the company has determined as the normal opportunity value or standard at which funds can and should be employed in the business.

For our example we will use 12 per cent. This will enable us to calculate the present value of all outlays and all inflows of cash. The resulting NPV represents an investment over the life of the project better than the companies standard. (The NPV Factors can be found in standard accounting NPV tables.)

	Year	0	1	2	3	4	5	6
£k	Cash flows	(100)	25	25	25	25	25	25
	PV Factors at 12%	1	0.89	0.80	0.71	0.64	0.57	0.51
£k	Present values (PV)	(100)	22.3	19.9	17.8	15.9	14.2	12.7
£k	Cumulative PV	(100)	(77.7)	(57.8)	(39.9)	(24.1)	(9.9)	2.8

18

Creating Commitment

When to use
When embarking on a project which requires commitment from a team of people.

What you get
A framework around which to design people's involvement in a project to maximise commitment.

Time
There are two time elements to this: the planning for commitment creation and the duration of the project itself. The planning should take about half a day.

Number of people
A selection of people who are going to be involved in the project. More than 10 would be difficult to manage.

Equipment
Somewhere to capture the output.

Method
1 Highlight the project and ensure that there is common understanding of the scope and objectives.
2 Explain how a committed team could help the project through to completion.
3 Go through each key factor in turn and discuss how to deal with each aspect of commitment to the project.
   Individuals join of their own free will: members should be volunteers not conscripts.
   The role of uncertainty: before a project can begin, employees need to be freed from their commitment to the past.
   Start small and build up: introduce new ideas gradually to allow individuals time and space to adjust to them.
   Joining requires an individual effort: involvement should appear attractive, exciting, challenging and rewarding. It should not be seen as the easy option.

Public acts of commitment: those who are committed and those supporting them must be announced both verbally and in writing.
Active involvement: active involvement must start early if people are to feel they can influence the outcome.
Clear messages and lines of communication: Communication should not be left to chance, build in effective mechanisms from the start.
4 Agree on a way forward to manage people's involvement in the project, considering each of the factors. Note them on the table shown opposite.

Example
See page opposite.

Exercise
Consider an example from your past where there have been exceptionally high levels of commitment and note things done before, during and after the project to maintain the levels of commitment.

Key points
Commitment can be a powerful force in change. It can provide the motivation and energy to achieve extraordinary results.

Additional comments
This is not a definitive solution in itself. It offers a summary of factors found to significantly influence levels of commitment in a project.

If high commitment is achieved it is important to do things to enable a reintegration with 'life as normal' when the project ends. Failing to do so can have painful consequences.

Other information
Example reprinted from R. Burgess and S. Turner, 'Seven key features for creating and sustaining commitment', *International Journal of Project Management*, **18**, 225–233, Figure 3, 2000, with permission from Elsevier Science.

Key commitment factors	Time		
	Before the project	**During the project**	**After the project**
Free will to join or leave	Free will to join	Free will to leave, but not rejoin	Freedom to become committed after the act
Role of uncertainty	Increasing certainty		
Start small and build up	Increasing levels of buy-in		
Joining requires an individual effort	Creation of elitism based upon individual input	Management of the potential them and us syndrome	System to reintegrate team members after the project
Public acts of commitment	Demonstrated commitment from others, especially senior executives	Demonstrated commitment from team members and those that will be affected by change	Recorded commitment and appreciation
Active involvement	Increasing scale and scope of involvement		
Clear messages and lines of communication	Communication of expectations and goals	Open and free communication of ideas, problems and feedback	Feedback and corporate learning

Key commitment factors	Time		
	Before the project	**During the project**	**After the project**
Free will to join or leave			
Role of uncertainty			
Start small and build up			
Joining requires an individual effort			
Public acts of commitment			
Active involvement			
Clear messages and lines of communication			

19

Critical Path Analysis (CPA)

When to use

In project planning to make worst and best case projections for completion. Also for analysing which elements of a project are the critical ones in terms of determining the length of time for the project.

What you get

A graphical representation of a project showing the necessary sequence of tasks and those tasks that can be done simultaneously. It also calculates the 'critical path' which is the series of tasks that determine the shortest possible project completion time. As such, this path needs to be carefully monitored and managed.

Time

Varies depending on size of project and level of detail. Although, with team involvement, a rough guideline could be created in 2–3 hours.

Number of people

Ideally the team of people who are responsible for the project.

Equipment

A large visible work surface suitable for writing on. A large number of copies of the task template, which is shown opposite.

It is important to keep it fairly high level to begin with, further subsystems can be added later.

Method

1   Assemble a team of people who are going to be responsible for the delivery of the project, and have knowledge of the subtasks that will be contained in the project.
2   Brainstorm or document all of the tasks that are needed to complete the project.
3   Identify the first task that needs to be done and record it on the far left of the work surface.

4   Question, 'Are there any tasks which can be done simultaneously with Task 1?' If there are, place these tasks above or below Task 1.
5   Identify the next task to be done.
6   Repeat steps 4 and 5 until all of the recorded tasks are in sequence or in parallel.
7   Number each task and draw connecting arrows to show the links between tasks. Finally, agree on a realistic completion time for each task, and record it on each task's template.
8   Determine the project's critical path. This can be done in two ways:
    Longest cumulative path: calculate the shortest possible completion time for all of the paths through the project. The path whose best completion time takes the longest time is the critical path.
    Calculated slack: this requires you to look at each of the tasks in turn and identify the time elements shown below. For consistency use the four-box grid to capture the times for each task.

Earliest start (ES)	Earliest finish (ES)
Latest start (LS)	Latest finish (LS)

ES = The largest EF of any previous connected task.

EF = ES plus the time taken to complete that task.

LS = LF minus the time to complete that task.

LF = The smallest LS of any connected following task.

When ES = LS AND EF = LF, that task is on the critical path, therefore needs to be highlighted

Making a cup of tea.

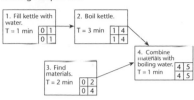

In this example, 1, 2 and 4 are on the critical path and therefore need to be monitored carefully.

■ **Exercise**

Complete a critical path analysis for going to work. Think creatively about how you could shorten the length of time it takes from bed to office, by considering things you could do simultaneously.

■ **Additional comments**

Can also be called activity network diagram (AND). There are a number of software solutions that can aid the development of the CPA. However, beware of over-complicating things with redundant 'functionality'.

Task No:

Task Name:

Time to do task:	Earliest start (ES)	Earliest finish (EF)
	Latest start (LS)	Latest finish (LF)

20

Cultural Audit

When to use
When embarking on a change project. For example, it is particularly useful when merging different companies or when partnering or entering into an alliance with a company.

What you get
A snapshot of the declared culture within an organisation, i.e. the 'way things are done round here'.

Time
Depends on size and scale of the audit.

Number of people
To design and carry out the culture audit a team of about five would be sufficient.

Equipment
A means of developing the design and capturing findings of the audit and somewhere to publish the findings.

Method
1 Be clear about *why* you are undertaking a culture audit, and *what* you intend to do with the findings. This will provide the basis for explaining to others the background and the design of the questions.
2 Select a mechanism for carrying out the research, two common methods are:
   Questionnaire: provides access to a wide cross-section of people in a fairly consistent way.
   Interview: provides more depth to the research, however, limits the numbers. Think about which approach would be more appropriate to your situation.
3 Identify specific areas for research, based on what you are trying to achieve.
4 Identify a broad selection of people from whom you can find the information.
5 Develop the interview/questionnaire.

6 Test the interview/questionnaire on the rest of the team or other 'safe' people, and make modifications, particularly focusing on areas of confusion, misinterpretation of question etc. It is also worth testing the analysis of the results. Do they fulfil the initial requirements of the audit?
7 Carry out the research.
8 Analyse findings.
9 Agree on actions as a result.
10 Get the organisation to accept the findings and buy-in to the actions.

Example
Analysing two different companies prior to their merger, to identify areas that may cause problems prior to them occurring so that pre-emptive action can be taken. The results from the questionnaire can be seen opposite.

Exercise
Consider creating a culture audit with the intention of increasing motivation in your area.

Key points
Different approaches are required for different situations.

There are many different factors that affect culture. Do not assume that all parts of an organisation have the same culture.

Taking a culture audit can be an effective way to monitor changes in culture during change projects, i.e. the culture before compared to the culture after.

Culture audits can be used at many levels, the key is understanding what you hope to gain from the exercise.

There is no right or wrong culture. Some cultures may just be more appropriate in some circumstances.

Additional comments
It could also be used when applying for jobs in companies, e.g. you could identify a culture that you want to work in and ask the people who are interviewing you questions that will give you some insight into the company. However, this will only be their view of the company and may not be a true representation.

If the audit is going to require other people investing time in it for you, prepare a justification in terms of what is in it for them prior to starting the interview or questionnaire.

There is a large amount of literature on the subject of organisational culture. A good summary of the major elements can be found in C. Handy, *Understanding Organisations*, Penguin Books, fourth edition, 1993.

■ Other information

Template

The statements set out below relate to organisational culture. They are not necessarily opposites, and there are no right and wrong answers. Consider each statement in turn and mark with an 'X' where this organisation lies.

	1	2	3	4	5	
Fast to change						Slow and methodical
Entrepreneurial						Stable steady
Reactive						Proactive
Management style empowering						Management style control
Dictatorial						Democratic
Secretive						Open
Creative						Traditional

Example

The questionnaire was sent out to 100 people across both organisation A and organisation B.

The results are summarised below. Company A's average ◯ Company B's average ●.

	1	2	3	4	5	
Fast to change		◯●				Slow and methodical
Entrepreneurial	◯	●				Stable steady
Reactive			●	◯		Proactive
Management style empowering	◯			●		Management style control
Dictatorial		●		◯		Democratic
Secretive					●◯	Open
Creative		◯●				Traditional

The two areas that will require work to smooth the transition are the management style and the organisation's approach to change. Work groups would need to be set up to address these issues prior to merging the two companies.

21

Customer Focus

When to use
When refocusing the business or part of the business to meet with customer needs.

What you get
A framework which when worked through will enhance the ability to provide customer satisfaction.

Time
1–6 months is average. It may take much longer in large businesses.

Number of people
A project team of 5–7 people will drive the project. It will require input from all parts of the business that the project touches as it goes through the framework.

Equipment
Place to display project status.

Method
1 Identify customer need: assume the customer requires the functionality of the product rather than the product itself. Model and understand the customer in depth. What problem are they trying to solve? Develop a complete set of functionalities and constraints to set the goals for success for the rest of the process. This stage requires substantial investment. Ensure the requirements are true and accurate.

2 Find a way to satisfy the need. This is the major thinking and decision-making part of the model. Its outputs are:
- The design of the product of the overall process. (This may be a physical product or could even be the business itself.)
- The definition of the processes that must be carried out to transform the starting material into the product or service.
- The definition of the material that must be acquired to be transformed.
- The definition of the means that must be acquired.
- Instructions for use of the product.
- The plan of what to do.

3 Winning an order. The 'process' or business is displaying to the customer that the required functionality, in total, has been understood and the proposed product and plan will satisfy the need, i.e. more than answers the 'question' posed by the 'identify' step.

4 When the plan starts to be enacted. All the things required, the material and the means, are acquired ready for use.

5 Purely the enactment of the instructions to transform the material into product in accordance with the instructions.

6 The delivery of satisfaction. This may include the delivery of the product or service but it is also the delivery of the functionality where, when, and how, required, to the quality required, and for as long as required.

Example
For a project to write this book.

Identify customer need	Useful, practical range of management tools at their finger tips
Find a way to satisfy need	A book, quick to find information, easy to use
Win order	Get commitment from publisher, author
Acquire the means	Research, knowledge, books
Transform the material into a product	Write the book
Deliver satisfaction	Publish and sell.
Measure degree of satisfaction	Revise future editions based on feedback

Exercise
Go through the process for getting photographs of someone.

Key points
Customers' needs constantly change, therefore it may be necessary to run the process regularly.

The model can be used at multiple levels in the organisations.

Remember the process is valid for internal customers as well as external ones.

■ **Additional comments**
Due to its simplicity, it is effective in many situations.

It assumes you know who your customers are.

■ **Other information**
Adapted from a model that was originally developed by the Project 2000 team at Rolls-Royce in 1990. Thank you to David Alexander for his help with this tool.

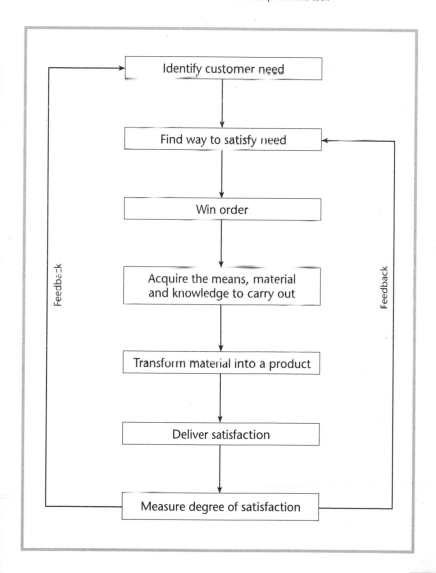

22

Decision Mapping

When to use
When you want to improve the decision-making process in a company.

What you get
A perspective of the business process in terms of the decisions taken within it.

Time
Depends on the complexity of the process product or service being analysed. Half a day should provide a useful insight.

Number of people
Involve a wide range of people involved and/or influenced by the decision process.

Equipment
Somewhere to map out the process: a wipe board or a large sheet of paper.

Method
1 Clearly define the decision process which is to be mapped, paying particular attention to its start and finish.
2 Break the process down into principal decisions and activities.
3 Create a high-level process map for them. For each of the decisions, identify:
   - information in and out of the decision
   - events that trigger the taking of the decision
   - constraints placed upon the decision
   - tools available to help in making the decision
   - people able to make the decision
   - how the taking of the decision is recorded

   Plot these on the map using the format opposite (it is the same format as used in Tool 64: Process Mapping – IDEF).
4 Having mapped the decisions in the process, consider what would help to improve the process, e.g. the timely arrival of information.
5 Create a set of actions to improve the decision-making process.

Example
Decision on what to eat for dinner.

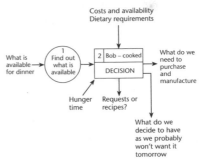

Exercise
Draw the decision map for choosing a route to work.

Key points
For effective decision making, it is necessary to take into account the following:

- The quality of the decision.
- The level of confidence in the decision.
- Time taken to arrive at the decision.
- The costs incurred in taking the decision.
- The timeliness of the decision.

Examples of actions taken to improve the decision-making process as a result of decision mapping are decision checklists and decision-making process guidelines.

Additional comments
Decision mapping is good for delays in processes due to poor decision making.
   Decision mapping can become over complicated, so it is important to keep it simple.

Other information
Original concept developed by, P. Davies, *Analyzing the Decision Points in Logistics*, Logistics Technology International, 1993, pp. 90–2.

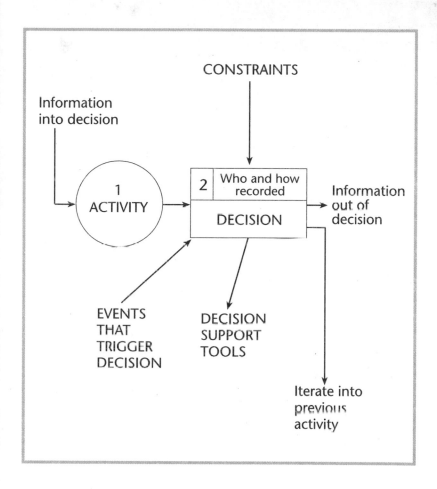

23

Decision Tables

When to use
When you need to select the best alternative from a number of options.

What you get
A rating score for each of the options based on appropriate criteria rather than 'gut' feel.

Time
Quarter-to-half-an-hour. More time might be necessary if you are trying to achieve a group consensus.

Number of people
Individually or with a group.

Equipment
Pen and paper or the template overleaf. A computer spreadsheet can also be useful.

Method
1. Construct a table as shown in the example. The left-hand column should list all of the options being considered.
2. The column heading should list the criteria by which you are judging each option.
3. These criteria should also be given a weighting factor to reflect their importance. You can decide to use more precise systems but we recommend using '1' for fairly important, '2' for important and '3' for very important.
4. The criteria main column headings each have three subheadings. One is for the score that the option gets for that criteria, the second is for the weighting value assigned to the criteria, the last is to record the product of the score multiplied by its rating.
5. Now work through each option in turn and rate it against the first criterion. Again you can use more precise systems but we recommend using '1' for very poor, '2' for poor, '3' for average, '4' for good and '5' for very good.
6. Repeat step 5 for the remaining criteria.
7. Calculate all of the subtotals for score multiplied by weighting factor. Then add up all of the subtotals for each option.

8. The option with the highest score is the one you should select.

Example
Tool 32: Forced Combinations, shows an example of ideas created for a product to cool a room. These are now considered using a decision table. Assuming the product is to be for casual home use, the criteria used to judge them are:

- Ease of use/effort from user – very important.
- Likely low selling price – important.
- Low running cost – fairly important.

The products ideas were:

A   Handheld manual fan.
B   Electric desk fan.
C   Air-conditioning unit.
D   Block of ice.

Option	Use Score	Weighting	Subtotal	Price	Weighting	Subtotal	Running	Weighting	Subtotal	Total
A	2	3	6	5	2	10	5	1	5	21
B	4	3	12	4	2	8	4	1	4	24
C	5	3	15	1	2	2	3	1	3	20
D	1	3	3	4	2	8	4	1	4	15

Based on the selection criteria the best option is B, a simple electric desk fan.

> B scores well in the two main criteria.

Exercise
Construct a decision table for choosing where to take someone to eat on a first date. The choices are: a burger bar, a fish and chip restaurant, a pub, a curry house and a posh French restaurant. You make up your own judgement criteria.

Key points
The table is a means of trying to arrive at an objective decision. It can also be useful, in a group, as a means of allowing people's issues to be included in the decision-making process. However, don't assume that because numbers are being used it is a scientific and accurate measurement. The weightings and criteria scores will usually include less objective data.

▓ Additional comments

If several options are quite closely scored, it is sensible to complete more in-depth analysis of these top options before making a final decision.

Using a spreadsheet to calculate the totals allows you to quickly change criteria scores and weighting scores. This is useful to quickly review different scenarios and see how 'robust' the recommended decision is.

Option	Weighting	Subtotal		Weighting	Subtotal		Weighting	Subtotal		Weighting	Subtotal		Weighting	Subtotal	Total

24

Design of Experiments (DOE)

When to use
When trying to understand the effect of multiple input variables on the output from a process.

What you get
An indication of the relative effect of each input or mix of inputs on the output, through a relatively small number of tests.

Time
Dependent upon the number and complexity of experiments required.

Number of people
A team approach is advisable to identify relevant input variables and potential interactions.

Equipment
Relevant experimental equipment and an appropriate orthogonal test array (see opposite).

Method
1 Define the output to be tested and the variables that most significantly affect it. Ask the people who operate the process.
2 Determine if any interactions exist between the variables. For each interaction a separate input variable is created.
3 For each input variable, determine how many levels or values the variables should be tested at, e.g. high, low, medium settings, etc.

4 Select the smallest orthogonal array (see opposite) into which you can fit the input variables and the levels at which they are to be tested. Spare spaces in an array can be filled with potential interactions, or less likely variables, or left blank. You may find they are more significant than you thought!
5 Do experiments for each row of the array using the appropriate input levels for each input variable (as defined by the array). Measure the resultant outputs.
6 Sum the outputs for each level of an input variable and note the average value. From this, the effect on the output can be obtained for each of the inputs.

Example
Satisfaction of a chocolate bar is rated as a percentage (%). Inputs are quantities of chocolate, nougat and caramel. For each, levels of high and low are defined. No interactions exist between these variables, so for two levels (high, low), three inputs (chocolate, nougat and caramel), a Level 4 array is required, i.e. four experiments (see table below).

Averaging the outputs from the table gives:

$\text{Chocolate}_{low} = (10 + 5)/2 = 7.5\%$
$\text{Chocolate}_{high} = (80 + 70)/2 = 75\%$
$\text{Nougat}_{low} = (10 + 80)/2 = 45\%$
$\text{Nougat}_{high} = (5 + 70)/2 = 37.5\%$, etc.

Immediately we can see that a high level of chocolate improves satisfaction, whereas nougat levels make little difference.

Exercise
Conduct an experiment similar to the one above but for different recipes of coffee. Use the following variables: coffee powder, milk and sugar. Use high and low settings.

Experiment	Chocolate	Nougat	Caramel	Satisfaction (%)
1	low	low	low	10
2	low	high	high	5
3	high	low	high	80
4	high	high	low	70

Key points

The output must be measurable and the input variables controllable.

Use brainstorming to identify input variables and potential interactions between them.

Start with a wide band of variable levels and then home in on the best combination as you learn about the system.

To select levels, look at the current state of the variable and set one higher and one lower. If the relationship between the input and output is not linear, consider more than two levels.

Additional comments

After running an experiment, you can validate that all significant input variables and interactions have been considered. Set up an experiment that does not replicate a combination of levels already used. The expected output (μ) is given by:

$$\mu = \bar{T} + (input1_{level} - \bar{T}) + (input2_{level} - \bar{T}) \ldots$$

where $\bar{T}$ is the overall average of all of the experimental outputs.

Compare the actual output to μ. Any difference indicates that other factors or interactions are significant.

You can get deeper into the statistics to determine the significance of results.

Other information

For further information see: G. Taguchi, *Introduction to Quality Engineering*, Asian Productivity Organisation, 1986; G. Taguchi, *Experimental Design*, 3rd edition, Unipub, 1978 or K. R. Bhote and Adi Bhote, *World Class Quality*, Amacom, 1999.

Commonly needed orthogonal arrays

Level 4 (3 variables, 2 levels)

		Input		
		1	2	3
Experiment	1	1	1	1
	2	1	2	2
	3	2	1	2
	4	2	2	1

Level 8 (7 variables, 2 levels)

		Input						
		1	2	3	4	5	6	7
Experiment	1	1	1	1	1	1	1	1
	2	1	1	1	2	2	2	2
	3	1	2	2	1	1	2	2
	4	1	2	2	2	2	1	1
	5	2	1	2	1	2	1	2
	6	2	1	2	2	1	2	1
	7	2	2	1	1	2	2	1
	8	2	2	1	2	1	1	2

Level 9 (4 variables, 3 levels)

		Input			
		1	2	3	4
Experiment	1	1	1	1	1
	2	1	2	2	2
	3	1	3	3	3
	4	2	1	2	3
	5	2	2	3	1
	6	2	3	1	2
	7	3	1	3	2
	8	3	2	1	3
	9	3	3	2	1

25

Diffusion of Innovation

When to use
When introducing a new product, service, process or project.

What you get
A discussion based around the timeframes of adoption of the new entity and the sizes of markets at each stage of adoption.

Time
1–2 hours will provide a useful insight.

Number of people
2–10 people who have an understanding of the 'new' entity. The involvement of stakeholders, customers and suppliers in particular can be very valuable.

Equipment
Flipchart or wipe board to capture the developments.

Method
1 People have different adoption rates; some like new things, some only purchase tried and tested products. It is important when considering launching something new that you consider the market in which it is entering and the speed with which it will travel from new to commonplace. The diagram opposite highlights the pattern associated with the diffusion of innovation, and the relative size of the market at each stage. The names given to the purchasing groups in each of these stages are summarised in the following table.

Type of purchaser	Description
Innovators	Like buying into new things because they are new
Early Adopters	Buy in a little later, after a few other people have tried it
Early Majority	Buy in after the initial hype
Late Majority	Buy in when they are confident that enough other people have bought in
Laggards	Buy in when nearly every one else has

2 Plot where your products or projects are on the diagram.
3 Consider the speed at which the products can travel through the diagram.
4 Look at how you can advertise, market and sell to these different categories of people.
5 Develop a plan to incorporate the elements discussed.

Example
When introducing a new brand of beer to the pub.

(a) Innovators – types of people that will try anything just because it's new, therefore it needs to highlight its newness in its advertising.
(b) Early Adopters – notice it's new but will probably try a little but have a regular pint as well. Allow tasters to encourage trial.
(c) Early Majority – 'If Bob drinks the beer, it must be OK.' Remove the emphasis on the newness of the drink.
(d) Late Majority – 'If everyone else is having one, go on I'll try it.' Put it on display where the best sellers are normally located.
(e) Laggards – 'I'll try it. It must be OK because you're still selling it.' Stop selling the old beer.

Timeframe: 1–2 weeks.

Consider the concept of diffusion of innovation for the introduction of an electric car.

What you do with the information is what makes it valuable.

If using it in a change process, It is important to manage people's involvement. Generally people's acceptance of the new will follow the same profile.

Consider overcoming barriers to adoption using Tool 34: Force Field Analysis.

■ **Additional comments**
Not all new things naturally follow this innovation cycle. It is a successful innovation cycle and the information is useful when preparing for an innovation's introduction.

Although people do have a natural adoption level, there maybe other factors that affect adoption rates of specific products and ideas that also need to be taken into consideration.

The impact of failure at each stage of the adoption process is also an area that may need to be taken into consideration.

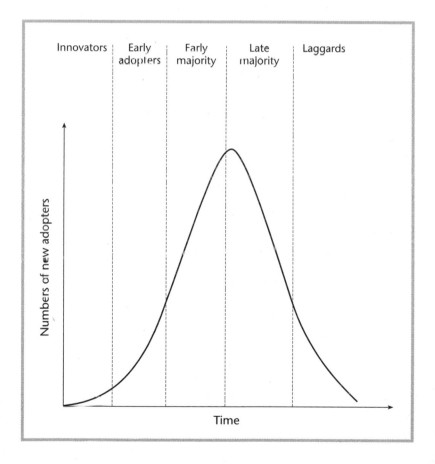

26

Effort Impact Graph

When to use
When you need to select the best from a number of options or projects.

What you get
A prioritised list of options.

Time
20 minutes depending on the number of options and the detail of the analysis.

Number of people
6–10 is about right. Fewer will compromise the accuracy of the process; more makes it unwieldy.

Equipment
Somewhere to list the options being considered and to show the effort impact graph. You can use the template opposite, a large wipe board or graph paper if you want to be more precise.

Method
1 List the options/projects being considered.
2 Explain that you are going to classify these options by (i) the impact or benefit they provide, (ii) the effort they will take to design, build and implement. Effort can be rated in terms of time, money or a combination of both.

> Benefits can be more than just monetary values.

3 Work through each option in turn asking the group to rate them as high, medium or low against impact and effort. When a few options have been placed on the graph you can use these as reference points for subsequent options, e.g. is option 5 more or less effort than option 2?

4 When all options have been placed on the graph allow the group some time to ensure that they are happy with the final positions.

5 Use the graph to prioritise the options. You should start with those that offer the greatest impact for the least effort.

6 As a guide, start with the options in the top left of the graph. If after achieving these options, the company is still resistant to change then select options in the bottom-left next. If however, the company is embracing change, build on the momentum by selecting options from the top-right next. Leave the bottom-right until last.

Example
The following example shows a number of ideas for promoting a new range of management books. These ideas now need to be prioritised.

The ideas, in no particular order are:

1 Write to everyone who might buy one.
2 Advertise in the specialist press.
3 Launch a major TV advert campaign.
4 Advertise on national radio.
5 Etc. . . .

Placing these on the graph gives the following.

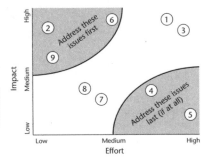

Based on this, efforts should first focus on option (2) advertising in the specialist press, followed by options (9) and (6). It is unlikely that options (4) and (5) will be used at all.

Exercise
List your transport options for getting to the shops and map them in term of effort (time, money, convenience) for you and their impact on the environment (pollution, congestion). What's the best way to be environmentally friendly?

■ Key points

The tool works best at the start of a major project when the options being considered are projects in their own right. At this point there is usually little hard information on which to base decisions. This tool allows the gut feel of experts in the area to be used to reach a consensus.

■ Additional comments

If accurate data is available, then the options can be plotted more accurately on the graph, e.g. impact might be measured as time or money saved.

Alternatively, the group can be asked to rank the options in terms of effort and then rank them again in terms of impact. The two ranking values can be used to plot the options.

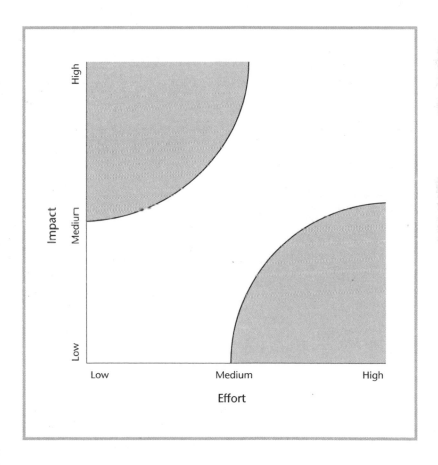

27

External Analysis (PEST)

When to use
At the start of a strategy review process.

What you get
An overview of the environment that your business is in, the factors that might affect it and hence issues that should be addressed in the strategy.

Time
Useful insight can be gained in about an hour. More time will be needed for in-depth analysis.

Number of people
The core strategy team. It can also be useful to seek input from outside of the organisation, i.e. from customers, research institutes, government statistics or consultants.

Equipment
A wipe board to capture ideas.

Method
1 Explain why you are running the session, what you hope to get from it and what it will be used for.
2 Brainstorm factors under each of the PEST headings – **P**olitical, **E**conomic, **S**ocial and **T**echnological trends.

> *Some people add an extra 'E' for environment.*

3 Discuss these factors and decide which are likely to have a significant impact on your business and its strategy.
4 If necessary, allow time to research these factors and gather relevant information.
5 Summarise the information ready to feed into the next stage of your strategy development process.

Example
Factors that might be relevant to the headings are:

Political: is the situation stable, is there an election soon, can we lobby government, are there any legislative changes on the way, are we significant to the monopolies and mergers commission, do we import from or export to politically sensitive countries, could our assets be seized, do our competitors have a good relationship with the government?

Economic: will the exchange rate affect our imports and exports, are company tax changes likely, how will interest rates affect our investments, will interest rates, taxes etc. affect our customers' purchasing habits, are suppliers and customers financially secure, what are our shareholders' expectations, do we need external finance for our strategies?

Social: do any of our business activities attract negative public attention, are there any trends that might threaten our existing markets or offer new opportunities, are there significant demographic trends, if we are not at the end of a supply chain do we understand who the end consumers are and what affects them?

Technological: what technologies might affect what our customers want, can we improve our internal technologies, do we have adequate training and investment to keep up with developments, what are our competitors doing, are there any developments that might reduce or erase the demand for our products, have we tried to exploit new technologies such as IT?

Exercise
Do a PEST analysis for a British car manufacturer. What are the significant issues?

Key points
The technique of PEST analysis is not clever in itself; it is just a checklist. However, it does help you to be thorough and logical in your initial analysis. Getting an accurate picture at the start of the strategic process increases the chance of developing a successful strategy.

The information from the PEST analysis can form the bulk of the 'Opportunity' and 'Threat' section of Tool 83: SWOT Analysis.

It is common for the technological trends to be overlooked during the analysis. This can be a mistake when you consider the current rate of technological development and the time horizon of most strategies.

Demographics are another source of information that is often overlooked. This is a waste as it is one of the more reliable sources of forecasting data.

■ Other information

See the other strategy review tools especially Tools 83: SWOT Analysis and 80: Stakeholder Analysis.

Political	Economic
Social	Technological

28

Failure Mode Effects and Criticality Analysis (FMECA)

When to use

When you have a system, product, service or process design to evaluate for safety. Done early to evaluate the safety criticality of a system, and in depth at the end to ensure safety issues have been covered.

What you get

A bottom-up systematic evaluation of the effects of failures in the system, a risk assessment and any requirements for system design.

Time

Depends on the complexity of the system. Break the system down into parts that can be analysed in 2–3 hours.

Number of people

4–8, including the design team, relevant experts and if possible an external.

Equipment

An FMECA chart and/or software package to capture information.

Method

1 Break down the system to its lowest components (usually outsourced, so ensure your suppliers provide their FMECAs).

It is good practice to have a diagram of how the system is broken down.

2 For each lowest-level component, look for any historical FMECAs to review. If none, a new FMECA is required.

3 Describe and document the component's functionality.

4 Brainstorm and record:
- all potential failures
- potential cause of failure

It is good practice to rotate through each member.

- existing controls against failure, detection mechanisms
- recommended remedial actions.

5 Calculate and record risk of failure:
- occurrence (O) or likelihood of a cause (1 = unlikely, 10 = almost certain)
- severity (S) of effect of failure on customer (1 = not significant, 10 = catastrophic)
- probability of detecting (D) failure so effect is avoided (1 = highly likely, 10 = almost impossible)

6 Calculate risk priority rating (RPN), the priority for corrective action:

$$RPN = O \times S \times D$$

7 Work through the system, from base-level components to top-level product.

Example

See opposite.

Exercise

Consider a troublesome system, product or process of your company and analyse its components parts to understand the source of the problem.

Key points

FMECA is a detailed and time-consuming task. So it is often used nearrds the end of the design cycle and applied to critical areas rather than a complete system.

Though commonly for faults and related safety risks, it is equally applicable to other risks, such as customer satisfaction.

It can also assist communication between all areas from design to production by bringing their input into the design process.

Additional comments

Other columns can be addes such as responsibility for taking action, and what actions were taken.

FMECA is different to HAZOP (Tool 37); it is a complementary technique, not a substitute. It is often used to provide information for a fault tree (see Tool 29: Fault Tree Analysis).

FMECA is an extension of Failure Mode Effects Analysis (FMEA), which does not include a formal risk analysis. FMEA is quicker to do, but does not provide a numerical ranking of areas with greatest need.

Other information

For more details see Neil Storey, *Safety Critical Computer Systems*, Addison-Wesley, 1996.

FMECA example – car radiator

Failure modes and effect analysis

Part	Car radiator
Functionality	The radiator removes heat from the engine coolant water by the action of a thermal transfer to cooler air passing through it

Item	Failure mode	Local effects	System effects	Potential causes	Current controls	O	S	D	RPN	Recommended action
1	Water freezes	Water does not move	Engine overheat due to lack of coolant circulation	Lack of antifreeze and sub-zero external temperature	None	3	6	8	144	Check antifreeze at 6 monthly service
2	Radiator housing split	Water leaks from radiator	Engine overheat due to lack of coolant	Water freeze expansion splits housing	None	3	6	8	144	Check antifreeze at 6 monthly service
3	As above	As above	As above	Impact damage	Grill filters air	1	6	8	48	Test that stones cannot hit radiator from below
4	As above	As above	As above	Manufacturing fault	ISO9001	1	6	2	12	None
5	Mounting loose	Radiator vibrates, potentially leading to mechanical failure	Radiator hits cooling fan and causes damage. Possible leakage	Mounting bolts not torqued correctly	None	2	8	8	128	Thread lock retaining bolts. Check radiator held at service
6	Water boils	Steam escapes from radiator	Engine overheat due to high water temperature and coolant loss	System blockage	Temperature warning lamp	5	8	2	80	None
7	As above	As above	As above	External temperature over 90 °C	As above	1	8	2	16	None

29

Fault Tree Analysis (FTA)

When to use
When you need to understand the root causes, or potential causes of a problem, or hazard.

What you get
A systematic graphical breakdown of the causes of a problem or hazard into a clear tree structure.

Time
Dependent upon the complexity of the system and depth of analysis required, nominally a few hours.

Number of people
For best results at least two people with relevant understanding of all facets of the system, process, product or service.

Equipment
A pen and paper for a basic FTA. Specific computer software is available for producing risk assessments based on the probability of each root cause.

Method
1 Clearly state the problem or hazard and place this at the top of a diagram.
2 Break the problem down into generic components or potential causes and place these in boxes below the problem in a tree structure (see example diagram).
3 For each connecting node in the tree, consider if the two linking components would cause the effect one level up the tree if they occurred independently (an OR gate) or if they are both required (an AND gate).
4 OR and AND gates are Boolean expressions, and are placed in the tree diagram at each node, denoted by the symbols:

AND   OR

5 Repeat steps 2 to 4 for each new block added until either no further cause can be established, or a consensus of agreement is reached that a sufficient depth of analysis has been undertaken.
6 Other symbols used in the tree are:

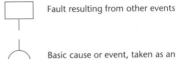

Fault resulting from other events

Basic cause or event, taken as an input

Cause event not fully traced back to its source

Example
The example is for a car radiator. The FTA can be seen opposite.

The analysis shows that if the system is low in antifreeze AND the outside temperature is low, then the radiator water freezes, which is a radiator fault. The radiator water being too hot also leads to a fault, but the manner in which the water gets too hot is not investigated.

Exercise
Consider the problem of a headache and try to break it down using a fault tree.

Additional comments
This analysis enables you to understand and map the connectedness of issues that normal, or more linear fault identification techniques would miss.

You can use other symbols for AND and OR if you prefer, e.g.

AND   OR

This tool is often used with Tool 28: FMECA.

Other information
For further detail see Neil Storey, *Safety Critical Computer Systems*, Addison-Wesley, 1996.

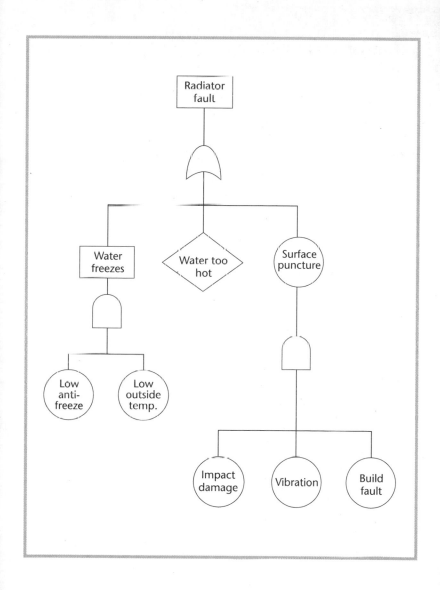

30

Five Whys

When to use
When you need to get to the root cause of a problem or gain greater understanding of an opportunity.

What you get
A number of different perspectives on the same problem or opportunity, which in turn gives you a broad base to contemplate subsequent actions.

Time
Anything from 5 minutes to 2 hours, depending on the size of the problem or opportunity.

Number of people
Varies depending on the problem, however, it is important to get a wide variety of perspectives. More than 20 would be difficult to manage.

Equipment
Large visible area to write on and capture the outputs.

Although it is called the Five Whys, Why can be asked as many times as is necessary to get to the root issues.

Method
1 Clearly define the problem or opportunity to be tackled.
2 Ask the group why? And capture the responses.
3 Continue to ask why until no more answers can be given.
4 Use the answers to identify actions that need to be taken.

Example
Shop sales have gone down. Why? People aren't entering the shop. Why? Alternatives are better. Why? Alternatives are cheaper. Why? No need to travel to shop to incur fuel and parking costs. Why? People can shop from home on the Internet. Why?

Exercise
Consider the problem of a door not closing smoothly.

Key points
This is a very simple technique that enables you to probe behind the obvious and explore other options.

It is based on the philosophy that a problem or defect provides an opportunity to understand fully the causes that led to it. Purely treating the symptoms denies the opportunity to fully learn about and deal with the root cause.

Additional comments
This tool's origin is primarily quality based. However, it is valuable in a wide variety of situations, enabling a greater understanding of the issue. This tool links to 16: Concept Fan and 10: Cause and Effect Analysis.

Success relies on people being open, honest and involved with the spirit of learning. If people are being defensive it is unlikely the findings will be useful. Sometimes the answers can branch off along a number of themes. In the example, there could have been two answers to the question 'Why are the alternatives better?' For example, 'cheaper' and 'more choice'. Both of these answers could then have been followed up by asking 'Why?'

Other information
Source: The Toyota Motor Company, who observed that asking 'why' five times normally established the root cause of a problem. However, it is a technique that children for many years have used to understand and learn about the world.

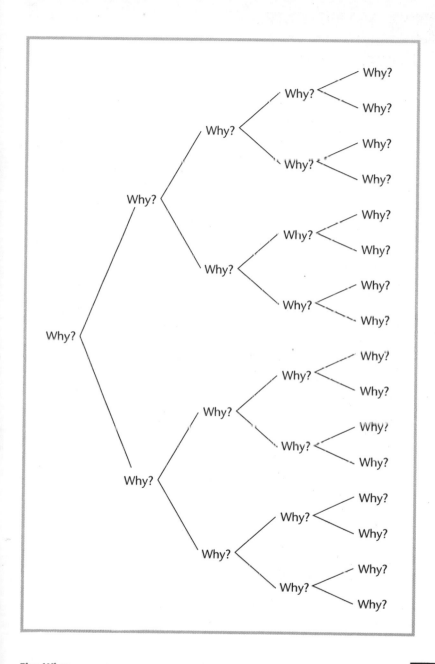

31

Flowcharting

When to use

When identifying and clarifying a flow or sequence of events in a process.

What you get

A picture of how the process is working.

Time

Depends on the complexity of the process being charted. For a high level overview, 1–2 hours would be sufficient.

Number of people

1–15 in the flowchart development session, ideally from across the organisation to give a broader perspective.

Equipment

Large visible area to capture and display the chart.

Method

1 Identify the process that is to be studied. Clearly state where it starts (inputs) and ends (outputs), and agree on the level of detail to use.

Flowcharting can be used as a first step in business improvement. You can then run two flow charts, 'AS IS' and 'IDEAL', then compare the two for areas where actions need to be taken.

2 Brainstorm the steps in the process.
3 Put the steps in sequence.
4 Draw the flowchart using the appropriate symbols.

Symbol	Explanation
⬭	Inputs or outputs of the process
▭	Task or activity
◇	Question or decision required
Ⓐ	Break in the flowchart to be continued elsewhere
──▶	Direction or flow of the process

5 Test the flowchart. Is this really what happens?
6 Discuss and agree actions to improve.

Example

A flowchart for producing a flowchart. See opposite.

Exercise

Create a flowchart for redecorating a room.

Key points

Flowcharting should be kept as simple as possible. Specific areas can be developed in more detail once the overall high-level picture has been agreed on. If appropriate, some of the major steps can then be expanded into separate more detailed flowcharts.

Always consider what you are trying to accomplish by developing the flowchart. This will help to provide focus when developing the chart.

Be consistent in terms of symbols used and level of detail.

Additional comments

Other useful variations on flowcharting are:

▪ Combining it with an input/output diagram. This helps to show the interactions between processes.

▪ Team integration to identify different roles and how and when they work together, and how ownership transfers throughout the process.

▪ Top-down, produce a top-level flowchart across the top of the page. Then add the details for each step below each of the top-level boxes.

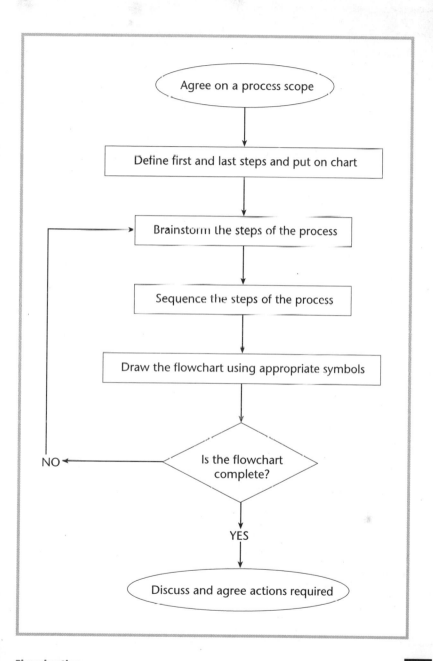

32

Forced Combinations

When to use
To bring structure to brainstorming and help logical people be more creative.

What you get
A list of possible design solutions.

Time
Varies greatly depending on the nature of the problems and the detail of solution being generated.

Number of people
Works best as per a small brainstorming session: 4–10 people.

Equipment
Plenty of space to write down ideas – flipcharts and wipe boards are best.

Method
1 State the design requirements in a manner that does not suggest a solution. For example, instead of saying we will design a new umbrella, the requirement should be stated as: we will design a means of keeping people dry while outside.

2 Break the basic requirement down into the major functions that the design will need to perform. Again, state these in non-solution terms. In the earlier example, a device for keeping people dry while outside, the main functions are (a) keep people dry, (b) be portable.

3 Now the group should brainstorm possible solutions for each of the functions. Usually, it is best to brainstorm each function individually rather than attempt to do them all at once.

> Use Tool 23: Decision Tables to evaluate ideas.

4 After the brainstorming has finished, the solutions should be recorded on a matrix.

5 The group can then attempt to make new complete designs using a combination of one solution for each of the functions. See the example for an illustration of this approach.

Example
In this case, the product requirement is for a means of keeping a room cool during hot weather. Breaking this down into the major functions for the product gives:

- Cool the air
- Move the air around
- Allow the user to control the temperature
- Operate using an available power source.

Each of these functions would then be brainstormed to create possible means of achieving them. Examples of the brainstormed ideas are shown opposite. The final stage is to consider combinations of these various ideas to make a complete product. Some common current products are shown to illustrate how these ideas could be combined.

Exercise
Use the technique to create ideas for products to allow people to access high-up places within the home. As the solution is for home use, it should also be easy to store away when not in use.

Key points
Similar to Tool 4: Brainstorming, don't do anything to stifle people's creativity. Allow and encourage all ideas to come out. They can be judged for practicality at a later stage.

Major functions are not the same as the criteria used for judging the design. In the example given, 'being safe' is a factor that will be used to judge the final designs but it is not a major function.

Forced Combinations

If the list of major functions grows beyond six the process usually becomes unwieldy, as there will be too many possible combinations to consider. A number of methods can be used to identify combinations:

- Work through each combination methodically one by one.
- Let the group brainstorm combinations.
- Let the group go away to think through the possibilities and then reconvene to discuss them.

At the combination stage, it can be useful to encourage people to make quick sketches of their ideas.

Sometimes it can be useful to look at an existing design to help understand what the functional requirements are. Although this can be dangerous as it leads people to think in existing ways and hence hinders creativity.

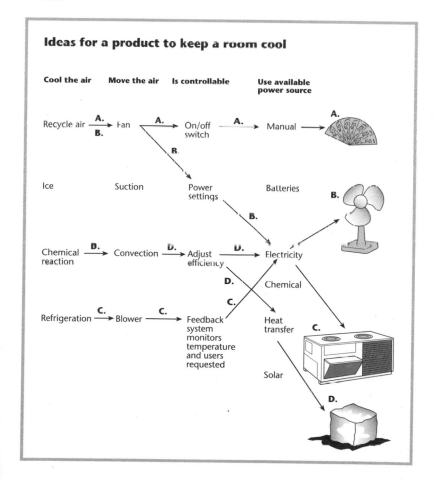

Ideas for a product to keep a room cool

Cool the air	Move the air	Is controllable		Use available power source
Recycle air **A.**	Fan **A.**	On/off switch	**A.**	Manual
		B.		
Ice	Suction	Power settings		Batteries
			B.	
Chemical reaction **D.**	Convection **D.**	Adjust efficiency **D.**		Electricity
			D.	Chemical
			C.	
Refrigeration **C.**	Blower **C.**	Feedback system monitors temperature and users requested		Heat transfer
				Solar

33

Forced Pair Comparison

When to use
When you need to prioritise a number of issues quickly. It is particularly useful when a group of people need to reach consensus.

What you get
A simple tally score as to the importance of issues relative to each other.

Time
Depends on the amount of discussion and the number of people involved. Normally 10 minutes to 1 hour.

Number of people
From 1–15. More than 15 would be difficult to manage.

It may be worth nominating a tally marker as well as a facilitator.

Equipment
A visible drawing (flipchart or white board) area with a simple spreadsheet drawn on. See spreadsheet opposite.

Method
1 Create a full list of options and place them in the spreadsheet.
2 Begin by selecting the top issue and ask the question 'Is option 1 better than option 2?'
3 Whichever is the better option; place a tally mark in the column next to it.
4 Then ask 'Is option 1 better than option 3?' and mark the better one with a tally.
5 Continue until you reach the end of the list, then take option 2 and repeat the process down the list, i.e. 2 better than 3? 2 to 4? 2 to 5? etc.
6 Continue this process for each of the options.
7 Add up the sum of tally marks for each option. The one with the most tally marks is the best option.
8 Calculate the relative positions of the options.

Example
Effective teambuilding options:

Options	Tally	Position
1. Organised team events	I I I	2
2. Understanding more about team members	I I I I	1
3. Nights out together	I I	3
4. Official team coffee breaks	I	4
5. More team meetings		5

The questions were:

• Is 1 better than 2? No (therefore mark 2).
• Is 1 better than 3? Yes (therefore mark 1).
• Is 1 better than 4? Yes (therefore mark 1).

And so on.
    The best option for this team was option 2.

Exercise
Do a forced pair comparison for holiday options.

Key points
Ensure that a tally is placed for every question asked.
    A facilitator is essential for groups of more than two to ensure speedy decisions are made effectively with the involvement of the whole team.

Additional comments
This method is very good at very quickly identifying priorities. However, it does not take any other issues into account other than people's preferences, for example the costs associated with options. If you are looking for a tool that allows for the effort associated with an option, see 26: Effort Impact Graph.
    The facilitator also has to be aware of 'louder' group members dominating the decision-making process. This can also isolate quieter members and risk losing their support. To prevent this, a formal raised arm or Post-it™ note voting system can be used.
    However, the simplistic nature of the tool should enable decisions to be made quickly, and objectively.

Forced Pair Comparison

Options	Tally	Position

34

Force Field Analysis

When to use
When planning to implement a change.

What you get
A simple visual representation of the factors that will aid the change and those that could hinder it.

Time
About 1 hour will give a thorough representation of issues.

Number of people
Anything from 1 to about 15. Doing this in a group will be of increased value due to broader range of perspectives.

This should involve people who will help be key drivers and key hurdles to the change.

Equipment
A white board or flipchart, a visible writing area.

Method
1 Identify the change that is to be considered.
2 Draw up a force field proforma (see opposite). Put the driving forces on the left and the restraining forces on the right.
3 Brainstorm (Tool 4) the driving forces and the restraining forces of the change.
4 Develop understanding of these issues through discussion.
5 Use the findings to put actions in place to maximise the driving forces and overcome the restraining forces.

Example
Changing a company's name.

Driving forces →	← Restraining forces
Desire for new image →	← Current brand
New leaders →	← 'Old school' in company
New culture →	← Customers' unfamiliarity
Inappropriateness of current name →	← Need for new stationery
	← Obsolete business cards
	← Legal formalities
	← Market place visibility and perception of stability

Exercise
Complete a force field analysis for moving house.

Key points
If the restraining forces are stronger than the driving forces then the change will not happen.

It is the strength of the forces that will determine whether changes will happen or not, not the number of factors. A way to get a very rough feel for the strength of the forces would be to ask the question in the session and mark the strong ones with, for example, a thick line.

Additional comments
It is important that action plans are created from the findings. This will create a key element of the change plan.

The act of asking people about their concerns for change and involving them in creating solutions is a very powerful tool in gaining their commitment.

Other information
Based on: Kurt Lewin, *Field Theory in Social Science*, New York, Harper Row, 1951.

Driving forces →	← Restraining forces

35

Forward Measurement

When to use
When the benefits from a project or proposition are more than just financial. Must use at the beginning of a project.

What you get
A framework for developing a measurement system that is based on both financial and non-financial measures in relation to a desired future.

Although some of the measures are less tangible they can still provide useful measures, i.e. you can feel if the atmosphere is friendly or not.

Time
4–6 hours will provide you with a set of measures.

Number of people
Ideally most of the people who will be involved with the project, and certainly those who are to be responsible for the delivery of the project. More than 15 would be quite difficult to manage.

Equipment
Somewhere to capture the outcome of the session, a wipe board or flipchart.

Method
1. Create a clear picture of what the 'ideal outcome' from the project would be. How would you be able to tell if you were at this ideal outcome? Consider all of the elements both financial and non-financial. How would things look, feel, appear etc?
2. Understand clearly *why* you want to measure, i.e. for learning, acknowledgement, contribution or value creation. Brainstorming would be useful here. Keep the output from this stage visible, as it will be a reference point for the measures that are developed.
3. Identify which of the items highlighted in step 1 are the most important. Which are the ones that if you can't identify, you wouldn't believe the project was a success?

4. The elements that are identified in step 3 are going to form the basis of the measures. For each of them, check that if you measured them, you would achieve the aim of the measurement from step 2.
5. For those that are suitable, if possible, put a timeframe on the measures.
6. Determine the actions that are necessary to achieve the outcomes. Continually reassess if the ideal is still appropriate and where you are in relation to that ideal.

Example
The ideal outcome from a successful supermarket shopping trip would be nice meals and a relaxed person.

The reason for measuring is to compare a number of supermarkets to see which one is 'best'.

A successful supermarket shopping trip would mean purchasing the correct high quality products, in a friendly environment, with easy local parking, in a clean shop, and within budget.

Exercise
Use forward measurement to measure the success of a dinner party.

Key points
- Based on measurement for learning rather than control.
- Flexible to changes, i.e. if the ideal outcome changes, the measures do also.
- Focuses action and intentions towards the ideal outcome.
- Anchors people in the future rather than the past.
- It is possible to use it at a number of levels.
- Need to check that the measures provide a balanced approach and do not create any unwanted side effects.

Additional comments
People may find it difficult to accept the sometimes less accurate yet fundamentally important non-financial measures. This may take some time for the organisation to have confidence in.

If the project requires external financial investment, it is unlikely that they would be happy with forward measurement in isolation. A traditional financial justification would certainly be necessary, also see Tool 17: Creating a Financial Business Case.

This tool has been found to be particularly useful for technology introductions, as it shifts the emphasis from financial return to desired outcomes.

■ **Other information**
Adapted from S. Turner, Towards Successful Technology Introductions, Executive Summary, Engineering Doctorate, 1998.

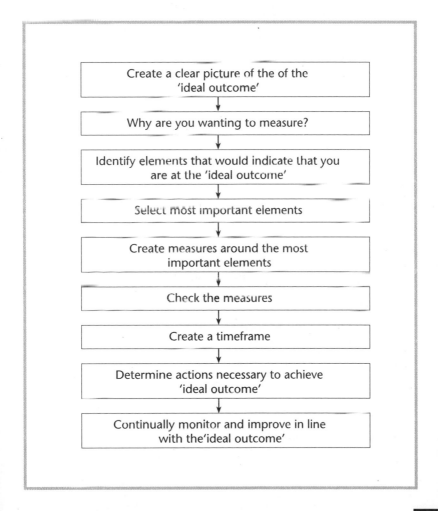

36

Gantt Chart

When to use
When creating a project plan, and/or monitoring progress.

What you get
A simple graphical representation of the plan which illustrates the tasks required, their progress and dependencies.

Time
Allow an hour to develop the chart plus planning time.

Number of people
One person to create the chart, but key players in the project should co-develop the plan.

Equipment
Paper, pen and a ruler for a handwritten chart (special planning paper or software can simplify the process).

Method
1 On a sheet of paper or spreadsheet create a grid with equal time slots across the top and tasks to be completed during the project on the left. See opposite. Set the time intervals according to the length of the project.
2 Break the project into tasks that are necessary to achieve the desired outcome and list these in chronological order on the left (note – it doesn't matter if tasks are concurrent).
3 Working from the top of the grid, identify the start date, and estimate the duration for each task. Draw a rectangle on the grid aligned to the task, which starts at the start date and extends to the right according to its duration and the time scale across the top of the chart.
4 Where the task starting is dependent upon the completion of another task, draw an arrow from the end of the required task to the start of the dependent task, see opposite.

5 To monitor the project status at any time, draw a thick horizontal line through the task rectangle, starting from the left. The length of this line in relation to the rectangle indicates the progress of that task (as a percentage of the task requirement). By drawing a vertical line through the current date on the chart timeline, tasks before the date that are incomplete are highlighted.

Example
The example opposite illustrates a plan to brew a cup of tea. Key features on the plan are identified.

Exercise
Use a Gantt chart to plan your next holiday.

Key points
You can work back from a delivery date to assess the feasibility of a project; this is called backward planning or right-to-left scheduling.

Be prepared for changes in the plan.

Look for critical paths, i.e. where dependencies could stop the project from being delivered on time. If these begin to fall behind, they will need to be addressed quickly. See Tool 19: Critical Path Analysis (CPA).

This tool ideally needs to be used in conjunction with 94: Work Package Breakdown.

Additional comments
Where you don't have a plan, the construction of a Gantt chart is a useful way to get one.

Other information
Concept originally developed in 1917 by H. L. Gantt.

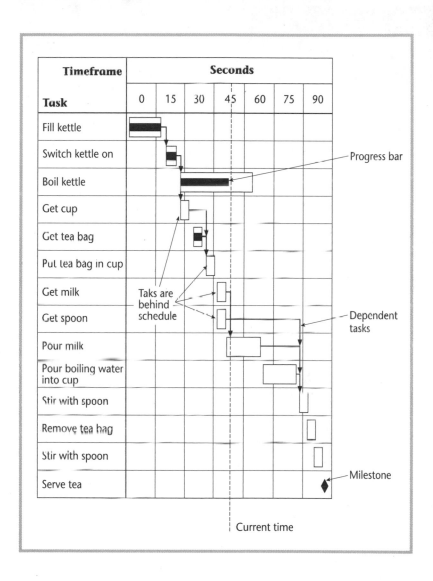

Timeframe	Seconds						
Task	0	15	30	45	60	75	90
Fill kettle							
Switch kettle on							
Boil kettle							
Get cup							
Get tea bag							
Put tea bag in cup							
Get milk							
Get spoon							
Pour milk							
Pour boiling water into cup							
Stir with spoon							
Remove tea bag							
Stir with spoon							
Serve tea							

Progress bar

Taks are behind schedule

Dependent tasks

Milestone

Current time

37

Hazard and Operability Studies (HAZOP)

When to use
Early in a design process (conceptual stage) to determine potential hazards related to a design.

What you get
A systematic evaluation of possible hazards, potential causes, consequences and design recommendations.

Time
Dependent upon the complexity of the system and depth of analysis undertaken, nominally 1 working day.

Number of people
4–8 people including experts in the area of the design as well as the design team.

Equipment
Pen and paper to capture the outputs.

Method
1 Break the system, product or plan down into component parts (depth required is based on expert opinion, but you can perform further HAZOP on components as required).
2 Consider how these components interact. 'Entities' pass between components, e.g. flow of materials or information from one area to another. Each entity has 'attributes', e.g. rate of flow of materials.
3 Systematically work through each connection between components in the system, identifying their associated entities. For each entity, determine its attributes. For each attribute consider any potential consequences of that attribute deviating from its correct value.
4 Record the potential cause and consequences of a deviation, and any recommendations arising for the design (see the example for a common documentation format).

Example
This example considers pouring water into a cup. The system is broken down into components and shown schematically below.

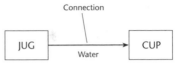

The results of a simple HAZOP on this system are shown opposite.

Exercise
Think of a system, product or process in your company, either currently in service or preferably being designed and carry out a HAZOP to identify any potential hazards of the system.

Additional comments
Guidewords help to identify ways in which an attribute may deviate from its normal state. Common guidewords used are:

No	e.g. **no** flow
More/Less	e.g. **more** flow than normal
As well as	e.g. a open **as well as** b
Reverse	e.g. **reverse** direction.
Maximum/Minimum	e.g. **max** possible value
Early/Late	e.g. signal arrives **early**
Before/After	e.g. signal a arrives **before** b
Faster/Slower	e.g. speed **faster** than normal
High/Low	e.g. **low** head count
Part of	e.g. **part of** delivery made
Other than	e.g. materials **other than** wool

These can be worked through systematically for each attribute of each interaction with justifications documented where they are ignored.

HAZOPs can be very tedious and time consuming. Software tools can help in both the documentation and running of a HAZOP. Try to break the system down into manageable 'chunks', so that the duration of any one sitting is not excessive. It often helps to have a system schematic in the documentation with an identifier recorded for each connection considered in the HAZOP.

▓ Other information

For further explanation see Neil Storey, *Safety Critical Computer Systems*, Addison-Wesley, 1996.

Item	Connection	Entity	Attribute	Guide word	Cause	Consequence	Recommendation
1	Jug to cup	Water	Flow	No	Jug empty	Cup Empty	Check jug full
2				Low	Jug not tilted	Long time to fill	Tilt jug
3				High	Jug over tilted	Cup might overflow	Level jug
4			Temperature	Low	Jug in cool place	Water might freeze	See no flow
5				High	Jug hot place	Cup might crack, or cause burn	Leave jug standing for 5 minutes

38

Histograms

■ When to use
When wanting to represent data in a way to understand frequency.

■ What you get
A graphical representation of data in a bar form.

■ Time
Depends on the time for data collection, the conversion into graphical form can be done either manually or using a computerised spreadsheet package.

■ Number of people
Only one to create the chart, it will require the involvement of others when considering actions to be taken as a result of the findings.

■ Equipment
Somewhere to capture the data, and to develop and display the chart.

■ Method
1 Determine the process that is to be monitored. (The data should be measured on a continuous scale, e.g. temperature, time, speed.)
2 Determine the approximate number of analysis groups.
3 Establish the upper and lower boundaries for the analysis groups. These must be equal in width. A simple way to calculate the width is: the largest observation minus the smallest observation divided by the approximate number of classes.
4 Create a table with the analysis groups down the side, and tally the observations, i.e. mark a tally in the relevant box when it is observed. When the time period for observation is up, add up the tally marks in each analysis grouping.
5 Plot the histogram. On the horizontal axis, mark up the analysis groups and on the vertical axis, add a scale for the frequency.

6 Analyse the findings. This can be done in a number of ways, summarised below are just a few:

Shape: the shape of the histogram may provide a useful insight into potential problems with the process.

Centre: if the chart displays a 'Normal' distribution, it may be possible to use the centre point of the chart as a lead into Tool 63: Process Control Charts.

Distribution: the spread of the chart will indicate the levels of variability in the data, again, this will be particularly useful if considering using control charts. It also gives an indication of process stability.

> Ensure there is no overlap between the analysis groupings.

■ Example

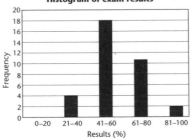

Histogram of exam results

Exam results

Results (%)	Tally	Total
0–20		0
21–40	IIII	4
41–60	HHH HHH HHH III	18
61–80	HHH HHH I	11
81–100	II	2

■ Exercise
Create a histogram for the number of telephone calls you receive during a day.

Histograms can be used to display the effectiveness of improvement efforts. It is particularly useful in the development of Tool 92: Vital Few Analysis.

Presenting data in a visual manner often helps to focus on the key issues. Histograms provide an indicator of issues; they offer no means for solving the issue.

It is possible to get heavily involved with statistics when analysing the charts.

■ **Other information**
Additional explanation can be found in basic mathematics books.

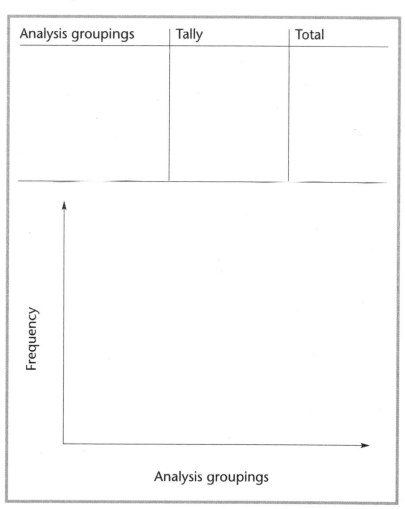

39

House Keeping – 5S

When to use
When giving your office or factory a sort out, or looking for productivity improvements. It is also sometimes called the 5Cs.

What you get
A set of actions to improve the overall productivity of an environment.

Time
To define and agree actions, 1–2 hours.

Number of people
Important to involve all of the people who are working in the area you are appraising.

Equipment
Flipchart or wipe board.

Method
1 Explain the background to the 5S:
The theory is that a tidy workstation, office or factory will improve productivity. The table below shows the English translations from the original Japanese words designed to focus attention on house keeping.

English – S	English – C
Sort	Clean up
Straighten or simplify	Configure
Scrub	Clean
Standardise	Conformity
Self discipline	Custom

2 Taking each section in turn, describe the essence of each of the 'S', and create a table similar to the one shown opposite and capture: what it means to your part of the business, who is going to be responsible for improving that area, and how you are going to measure improvements.

Alternatively, you can allocate separate groups to tackle each of the main headings.

Sort: Remove all items that are not required in the near future. It is worth setting a timeframe for the usability, begin with six months and gradually work it down to about a week. Consider things like, paper, memos, dirt, manuals, inventory, rubbish and tools. It is possible to 'mark up' items that don't move, using simple indicator systems for time left untouched.

Straighten: Put frequently used items in easily accessible places. Ensure everything is clearly labelled and easily identifiable. Colour coding is very practical.

Scrub: Keep things clean and ready to go. Don't wait until things are really dirty; keep on top of things by introducing preventative cleaning schedules.

Standardise: Create standards for each area. These need to be clearly visible and should cover both what to do when things are normal and also what to do if things go wrong.

Self-discipline: Comes from ensuring that the improvement activities are ongoing. Although the initial introduction will provide a sharp improvement, it is its ongoing use that provides the key to the most benefits.

Example

S – To Desk	Responsible	Measurement
SORT – in tray, paperwork, cups		Clean desk end of day, in tray 2 cm deep
STRAIGHTEN – filing system	S.T.	Number of files left out
SCRUB – copier, printer, game pack	P.F.	Damage limited
STANDARDISE – all housekeeping	S.T.	Check sheet conformity
SELF-DISCIPLINE – all house keeping	S.T.	Put reviews in place

Exercise
Use the 5S approach to your workspace.

Key points
This is an ongoing process of improvement. Management participation and interest is vital to this. Dramatic savings often result when 5S is introduced.

Additional comments
To encourage the technique, you can allocate people to certain areas. In this way they take responsibility and pride in the area where they work. This area becomes their second home.

Other information
Source: Toyota Motor Company. Further information on this tool can be found in H. Hiroyuki, *5 Pillars of the Visual Workplace*, Productivity Press, 1995 and H. Hiroyuki, *5 S for Operators*, Productivity Press, 1996.

S – In our business	Person responsible	Measurement
SORT		
STRAIGHTEN		
SCRUB		
STANDARDISE		
SELF-DISCIPLINE		

40

Improvement Cycle

■ When to use

When you need a framework for any kind of improvement.

■ What you get

A framework which is adapted for your own improvement process.

■ Time

Improvement is an ongoing process. To set up the framework will take 2–4 hours.

■ Number of people

1 or more, it is equally useful at a personal level as it is at a group level.

■ Equipment

The diagram opposite displayed somewhere visible and a flipchart or wipe board to capture the output of the session.

■ Method

1 **PLAN**

Understand –
Clearly define the problem/ process that is to be addressed.

> There are a considerable number of tools in this book that will support each stage of this process. See the project matrix for specific help.

Gain an understanding of what you are trying to accomplish.

Analyse – Understand the root cause of the issue. Define the current processes surrounding the issue and back up with useful information.

Organise – Develop the detail of what needs to be done.

Prioritise – Develop an effective and workable solution and action plan, including targets and people responsible for improvement.

2 **DO**

Implement the solution, ideally in pilot form to begin with. Follow the plan and monitor progress and learning points.

3 **REVIEW**

Review and evaluate the results of the actions. Are you getting the result you anticipated? What else is happening? What can you learn from the results?

4 **ACT**

Reflect on learning. Understand what needs to be done differently and act on findings.

■ Example

Problem: Being late for work.

PLAN: *Understand –* Aim is to get to work on time. *Analyse –* Having carried out a cause and effect analysis and plotted the impact of the causes on a vital few chart, it appears that the main cause of the delay is on one specific part of the route. *Organise –* Plot out other routes to avoid delay area. *Prioritise –* Select the best option.

DO: Time the journey using the selected route.

REVIEW: Determine whether it was a shorter time to work than previous route.

ACT: Consider now other areas of time reduction. Is the new route consistently better or are there other, better routes?

■ Exercise

Consider the elements of the improvement cycle for the problem of poor communication.

■ Key points

Often we do not spend enough time reviewing, reflecting and learning from what has gone on, always being too busy and needing to get on with the next thing. The Review stage is fundamentally important, as it will save time, effort and energy in the long run. The challenge is for managers to allow this to happen in all parts of business.

The most important thing that the cycle provides is a common language for continuous improvement. It is important to note that it is a cycle. Once you have completed the 'Act' stage you go on to the 'Plan' stage.

■ Additional comments

There are many frameworks for continuous improvement and problem solving; the simplistic nature of this tool enables it to be used in a large number of environments.

■ Other information

This tool is based on Deming's Cycle – for further information see www.deming.com or M. Walton and W. Deming, *Deming Management Method*, Perigee, 1998.

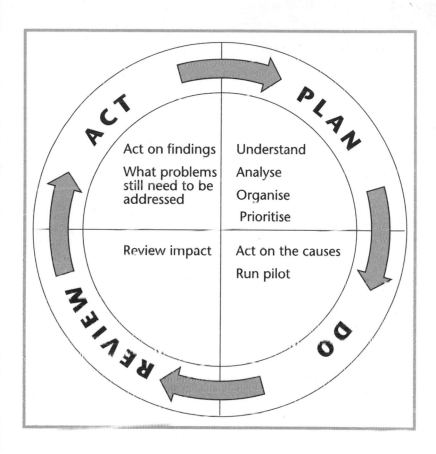

41

Improving Group Communication

When to use
When looking to improve communication skills in a group environment.

What you get
Personal feedback on how individuals communicate in a group and possible areas for improvement.

Time
2–4 hours will provide a thorough analysis and provide some time to practise new methods.

Numbers of people
10–16: it is important that you have an even number of participants.

Equipment
Pens and paper. Also a subject matter to discus or a problem to solve.

Method
1 Explain fully the subject or problem which is going to be addressed in the session.
2 Each participant needs to find a partner that they will feel comfortable getting feedback from. In pairs gain an understanding of the other's input to the subject of the session, looking specifically for strong opinions, additional facts, and desired outcome.
3 From each pair one person needs to join group (a) and the second person group (b).
4 Group (a) form an inner circle to begin the discussion and with group (b) creating an outer circle to be the first observers.
5 Set a time limit of 20 minutes on the discussion, in which time, the observers need to note how their partner participated. Noting specific instances and examples. Specific areas to look for are: clarity of point making, involvement of others, receptiveness to other's ideas, objectivity when questioned, question asking, and listening skills.

Ideally you decide on specific areas to focus on in terms of observation to provide a consistent means of feedback, an example of which is shown opposite.

6 Return to your partners and do a review of observations for 5–10 minutes.
7 Group (a) returns to the discussion with group (b) observing, for a further 10–15 minutes. Then repeat the review process focusing on the changes in behaviour.
8 Repeat steps 4–7 with group (b) in the middle and group (a) observing.
9 Work together as a whole group and continue the discussion.
10 Break out for one final review session with partners.

Example
This provides an extract from a feedback session.

'At the point when Jo was talking about her approach, it appeared to me that you disengaged, you started to look out of the window and started to fidget. In comparison when Claire was talking you appeared to become much more involved. When questioned on your approach it seemed to me that you became defensive and started to back track.'

Exercise
Begin by getting feedback from people close to you on how you dealt with a situation of organising a weekend away.

Key points
When giving feedback, do so objectively on what you witnessed.

Receiving feedback can be fairly painful, remember to listen to the feedback rather than trying to justify your behaviour.

There is no right and wrong way to behave in a group, this exercise is a way of improving working together.

Additional comments
Be careful, some people may see this as an opportunity to attack someone's personality; all feedback should be in light of helping individuals to improve their effectiveness in the group.

It is very hard to behave 'normally' when you are being observed. For the process to be effective, it is important that people are as natural as possible and don't over analyse their own behaviours.

Other tools for improving the way a group
interacts can be found in P. Senge *et al., Fifth
Discipline Field Book*, Nicholas Brealey, 1994.

Area	Observed behaviour
Listening	
Presenting information	
Involving others	
When questioned	
When challenged	
Questioning	

42

Influence and Control

When to use
When needing to focus down to a level that is appropriate and achievable.

What you get
A diagrammatic representation of where issues or opportunities sit in terms of the teams or the individual's ability to control and influence them.

Time
Half-an-hour should provide a fairly good indication of where the issues lie.

Number of people
1–15: specific numbers will depend on the type of issues being analysed.

Equipment
Wipe board or flipchart to capture the output.

Method
1 Agree the list of items that are to be considered. This could be change opportunities or personal concerns for example. Tool 4: Brainstorming will be useful here to flush out all of the issues.
2 Go through the list and consider for each one, can you or this team: influence and control the issue, influence and not control the issue or neither influence nor control the issue. For each issue place it on the diagram opposite.
3 Focus on the issues that are in the centre category, i.e. influence and control. These are the issues that need to be taken forward and actions put in place to sort out.
4 The issues contained in the next level of the circle, i.e. influence and no control. Use Tool 43: Influence Diagrams and Tool 59: Power Maps to increase the effectiveness of your influence on these issues.
5 The issues in the outer category, i.e. no influence and no control. Be aware of the issues, and the impact they may have on the issues you can control, but limit the time that is spent discussing solutions, as they will have no impact on what happens.

Example
When preparing for a marathon.

The issues to focus on first are sustenance, training, equipment and fitness. Minimal time and effort should be spent on the weather, distance and other competitors.

Exercise
Complete an influence control diagram for the issues facing the house that you live in.

Key points
Be realistic about what you actually have control and influence over. We often have less control that we believe. The boundaries will move, over time issues will move between groups.

If there is an issue that you currently have no control over, it is sometimes possible to influence people to enable it to move into the controllable category. Make sure you fully understand the reasoning for wanting to control the issue.

Additional comments
Be careful that too much time isn't spent debating the grey areas between the groupings. If they are grey, they are probably less important that those that are not.

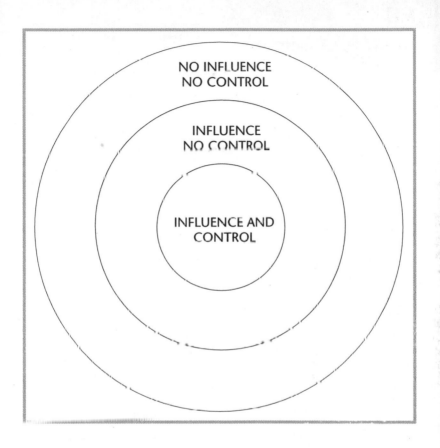

NO INFLUENCE
NO CONTROL

INFLUENCE
NO CONTROL

INFLUENCE AND
CONTROL

43

Influence Diagrams

When to use
When facing an issue or problem and a solution would benefit from understanding the factors that influence the issue.

What you get
A picture of multiple factors that influence the issue or problem, enabling you to get a thorough understanding of the situation prior to selecting a solution.

Time
2–4 hours depending on the complexity of the issue.

Number of people
Ideally a group of 4–6, larger groups can work if carefully facilitated.

Equipment
A wipe board or flipchart to capture the output of the session.

Method
1 Agree on a common understanding of the issue or problem to be discussed. Summarise in a short sentence.
2 Determine all of the factors that influence the issue or problem. A good tool to determine the factors is Tool 4: Brainstorming.
3 Arrange the factors in a circle on the flipchart or wipe board. Leave plenty of space between the factors for adding arrows later.

Start with one and work your way round.

4 Look for cause/influence relationships between each factor and connect them with arrows. If no relationship, do not put in an arrow. If there is a relationship the point of the arrow goes to the factor that is most influenced (not the one that influences). *Do not draw two-headed arrows.*
5 Check that the diagram is complete and accurate.
6 Tally the number of ingoing and outgoing arrows for each factor.

7 Redraw the diagram including the number of ingoing and outgoing arrows for each factor. Highlight the factor that has the *most outgoings* as the likely *driver* of the issue. Highlight the factor with the *most incoming* arrows as a key *outcome*.
8 Initially focus on the driver; this is likely to be your point of maximum leverage on the issue.

Example
See opposite.

Exercise
Complete an influence diagram for the issue of time management.

Key points
● Largest number of outgoing arrows – Key driver.
● Largest number of incoming arrows – Outcome.

The key driver is normally the one which if focused on will have the greatest impact on the outcome.

For a more refined approach it is possible to put a weighting on the arrows to indicate the strength of influence. This significantly increases the complexity of the tool.

The methodology behind influence diagrams can also be used to understand the influence relationships in a group of people. See Tool 59: Power Maps.

Additional comments
The diagrams often become over complicated and impossible to decipher. To minimise the risk of this, work with a maximum of 20 factors and only indicate major influences.

This tool does not provide you with a solution; it points you to the area of most leverage.

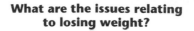

What are the issues relating to losing weight?

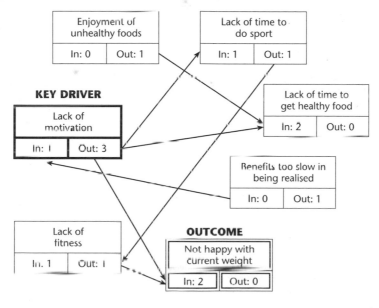

In light of the findings, the area to focus on to achieve weight loss would be motivation.

Note: There were two factors that had the maximum of two incoming arrows. If this happens use common sense to decide which one is the more likely outcome.

44

Input Output Analysis

When to use
When analysing activities, processes, information flows and problems. It can be used to analyse simple activities right through to complex business environments. It enables complex systems to be broken down into manageable subsystems.

What you get
A simple pictorial representation of an activity, broken down into its key elements.

Time
Varies depending on depth and complexity of activity being analysed. 1–2 hours should provide an initial overview of the activity.

Number of people
Depending on activity, 1 to about 12. To maximise value it is best to involve a selection of people who are involved in the activity being analysed.

Equipment
Visible means of collecting the information.

Method

Input	Activity	Output
Resources →	Processing and transformation activities	Requirements of the system →

1 Define the activity and write it in the activity box.
2 List all outputs from the activity and put those on the right.
3 List all inputs to the activity and put those on the left.
4 Consider any 'byproduct' outputs.

Example
Making a cup of tea

Water →		
Tea bags →	Making a cup of tea	A hot cup of tea →
Milk →		
Sugar →		
Cup →		
Electricity →		

Looking in more detail, you can break the activity down into subactivities, e.g. boiling the water, putting in the tea bag, milk, sugar and boiling water into a cup. 'By-products' in this example will be a used tea bag and probably steam.

Exercise
Produce an input output diagram for washing a car.

Key points
Input output diagrams may be linked together to show where inputs are used, where outputs go to and the interdependency of processes. e.g. To get an overview of a department, individuals complete an input output diagram for their role and then connect them together.

Additional comments
People can complete the diagram in any order rather than working through the stages. Some find it useful to start by thinking about subactivities within the main activity. The rule is: whatever helps think it through is acceptable.

Look for inputs and outputs that do not connect to anything else. Equally, look for inputs and outputs that are duplicated. These might indicate inconsistencies, and be areas for improvement.

As well as analysing current processes and activities, you can also work from a blank sheet of paper to design a new system. Start by deciding the required output, then define the inputs necessary to achieve it. This should ensure that only the essential elements are designed in.

For a similar but more detailed approach, consider using Tools 64: Process Mapping – IDEF or 89: Time Based Process Mapping (TBPM).

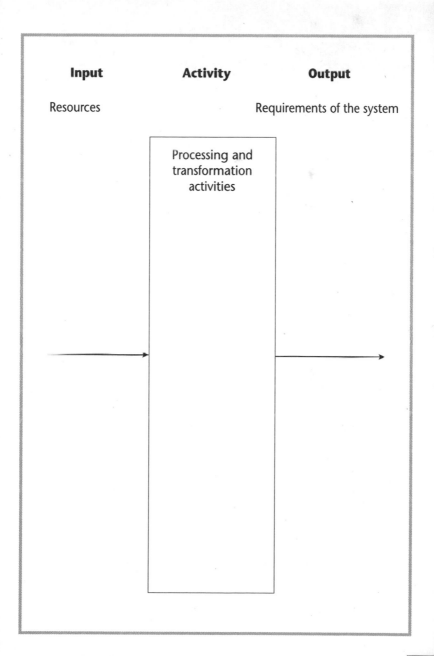

45

International Business Context

When to use
When doing international business.

What you get
Some areas to focus on to improve international business relationships.

Time
About 2 hours to do the preparation work.

Number of people
One person to do the research. However, everyone in your organisation who is going to be closely involved with the international business needs to be briefed.

Equipment
Checklist opposite.

Method
1 Research the countries that you are going to be working with. Use the checklist opposite to help structure the research.

You cannot over study the culture of the country in which you intend to trade.

2 Consider the impact of your findings on the business you are intending to conduct.
3 Adopt a strategy to optimise the relationship.

Example
Consider selling a new kind of soap to a group of children playing in the street. To break into their game, you would have to understand their language, the hierarchy of the group, what motivated them and how you could interest them in something alien to what they were doing. All of the issues of power, politics, sensitivity, motivation, and currency are in play.

Exercise
Consider selling this book in Brazil. What issues would you need to take into consideration? Where is it possible to find helpful information?

Key points
This tool can be used for all levels of business; it could be anything from the use of another of these tools with people from another country, to introducing a new product or service to an international market or opening an internationally based satellite business. Either way understanding the business context and ethics of different cultures will enable a more successful outcome for all involved.

Add other items to the checklist that are particularly pertinent to the country you intend to work with or in.

Additional comments
Using this tool will not guarantee international success; it will, however, provide you with information that will help when deciding on strategies to move forward.

Other information
The Internet is a good source of information on different countries. See also local embassies for help. See also Tool 46: International Etiquette.

Areas to research	
Area	**Findings**
Communications infrastructure	
Currency stability/tradeability	
Demographics	
Distribution facilities	
Economy and economic drivers	
Freedom of trade	
History	
Hours of business	
Involvement/Power	
Language	
Laws and legislation	
Literacy levels	
Military involvement	
Physical environment	
Politics and government	
Power sources	
Relationships with neighbouring countries	
Religion	
Safety	
Social priorities	
Tastes	
Taxation	
What is polite and impolite	
Other	

46

International Etiquette

When to use
Prior to conducting international business either in your own or another country.

What you get
Improved relations, respect and therefore business between the cultures.

Time
To prepare yourself should take no more than 2 hours.

Number of people
All of the people who are going to be representing your business in the international arena.

Equipment
Form shown opposite.

Method
1 Do some research on the country and culture you are going to meet with. The form opposite will provide a useful guideline. Detailed opposite are some general guidelines.

You could do the research for all of the countries you deal with and use them as an international briefing kit. Share them with the rest of the business.

Area	Guidelines
Dress	Appropriately and in keeping with their rules. If in doubt ask.
Introductions	Introduce the highest ranking person first. Adapt the formal greeting for that culture. Wait for the senior host to advise you where to sit at the meeting table.
Communication	Non-verbal communication is often remembered longer than verbal. Don't speak too quickly. Will an interpreter be necessary?
Timings	Different cultures work at different paces and have different expectations of timings – manage expectations through this.
Eating	Find out if any foods or drinks are 'unacceptable' either for religious or legal reasons. Check for any actions that could be construed as insulting.
Thank you	Gifts are sometimes expected, but could violate the company's ethics code or local law. A handwritten thank you goes a long way.

Example

Detailed below are some examples from different countries.

Dress	USA fairly casual, UK formal.
Introductions	European and Latin countries often kiss on the cheek.
Communication	Do not assume that if English is their first language people understand what you are saying, always check for understanding.
Timings	In some countries people are notoriously late. However, always turn up on time as a sign of respect.
Eating	Muslims do not eat pork or drink alcohol, and at a Muslim meal, never use the left hand to touch food. Buddhists do not eat beef.
Thank you	Americans and Japanese normally give gifts. US tip everyone.

Exercise

Imagine you are going on a business trip to Japan, what are the key things you would need to take into consideration?

Area	Guidelines
Dress	
Introductions	
Communication	
Timings	
Eating	
Thank you	

Key points

Don't assume that a whole country behaves the same, if possible find out about the specific area that they come from.

International etiquette is particularly important when visiting people in their own habitat.

Additional comments

Don't overdo it, be respectful of the culture not imitating, people may find this offensive. A little research can go a long way to successful international business.

Other information

There are a few books on the subject which provide useful summaries of the key points for each country, see R. Axtell, *Do's and Taboos of International Trade*, Wiley, 1994. Other information on different cultures can be found on the Internet, or by asking other people who have been to the country.

47

Just In Time (JIT)

When to use
A manufacturing tool which is useful when variety of product is high and system flexibility is key.

What you get
A system which pulls materials and products through the system based on direct customer requirements with minimal waste. Waste in this context can mean excess, lead-times, work in progress, capital employed, production, scrap, space and poor quality.

Time
JIT is a philosophy, not a task to perform. So it requires 100 per cent of people's time.

Number of people
The whole organisation needs to be involved. To get maximum benefits it is important it is not seen as just a 'production thing'. It extends beyond the traditional manufacturing boundaries to include sales, admin, finance, purchasing.

Equipment
No specific equipment is required.

Method
1 Outlined here is a high-level approach to JIT introduction. The page opposite offers an overview of the key elements that need to be in place before and during the introduction of JIT.
2 Learn about JIT and analyse its appropriateness for your business. JIT is a philosophy with a number of key elements, a summary of which is shown opposite. It may be appropriate to implement some or all of the elements. See Other Information for more help.
3 Create a multidisciplinary team to explore the whole business from supply chain through production to customer.
4 Create action plan to pilot the key elements.
5 Run the pilot.
6 Modify and improve. Capture and disseminate learning points for the roll-out plan.

7 Create roll-out plan.
8 Carry out roll-out.
9 Sustain continuous improvement cycle.

Example
A bar. (This example shows the pull system in operation.) In a bar if a push system was in operation before you entered the bar, the bar attendant would assess how many customers he would have on that particular day and how many of each type of beer, wine or spirits would be ordered, he would pour them all and then sit them all on the bar ready for the customers to pick up.

A pull system is based on demand. You walk in order a pint, one is poured instantly, you drink it and the bar attendant does not pour another one until you request it. Once again he pours it instantly.

In this simplified case the measurements in place were customer satisfaction and waste. The pull system won without question as the push system let the drinks go warm, and whilst there was a surplus of some drinks, others were out of stock, so the customer was unhappy. For the bar too there were benefits: in the first scenario if he incorrectly predicted the demand, waste in terms of stock out and overproduction would be incurred. This would not occur in the pull example.

Exercise
Consider the implications of reducing batch sizes on your next food-shopping trip. What factors do you need to consider? Which items have to be in large batch sizes? How much inventory can you afford to have tied up in your cupboard? How much waste do you have in the system?

Key points
● There needs to be top management commitment, involvement and leadership.
● It is imperative that people are trained in the JIT techniques and philosophy.
● The success of JIT implementations is down to the people.
● You have to work at JIT; it requires a change in behaviours and attitudes that will not happen overnight.

Additional comments
Do not expect JIT to provide a magic solution to business problems. Continuous improvement does work but you have to work at it.

Just In Time (JIT)

Other information

The summary below is based on J. Bicheno, *Implementing JIT*, IFS Publications, 1991. For further information see: R. Schonberger, *Japanese Manufacturing Techniques*, Free Press, 1982; R. Hall, *Zero Inventories*, Dow Jones/APICS, 1983; C. Adair-Heeley, *The Human Side of JIT*, Amacom, 1991.

Preparing for JIT

	Description
Team work	It is important to foster team spirit for improvement. Incentives and rewards need to be focused around improvement. Training will be key both in the JIT philosophy and tools as well as techniques to support the new business.
Quality	Build in quality processes. Introduce preventative measures to ensure quality. If a quality problem is found it is important to stop and address the root problem. JIT will not work with poor quality.
Maintenance	Responsibility lies with the operators and maintenance experts. Need visible charts to minimise maintenance surprises and enable preventative maintenance. Statistical control is fundamental here.
Demand	Work towards creating stable predictable demand. Work with customers to build trusting relationship to encourage smaller more regular orders – consider how to deal with 'rush jobs'.
Focus	Identify the products, resources and competitive advantage that are most important and concentrate attention on them.
Small machines	Consider using several small multifunctional machines instead of one big one. This will provide increased flexibility in a number of areas.
Layout	Need to consider waste minimisation and flexibility in terms of layout. House keeping is key.
Change-over time reduction	Reduce change-over and set-up times. Analyse practice and improve. Objective – to minimise set-up times to enable reduced batch size production.

Delivering JIT

	Description
Team involvement	Those close to the action are best qualified to make improvements. Encourage the sharing of ideas, and ownership of the improvement process.
Visibility	Highlight problems as they occur, celebrate successes, and simplify and make visible all measures.
Process data collection	Collect and use data as it happens. Create ways to minimise confusion and increase accuracy of inventory levels. Measure quality in the process and implement actions on identification.
Enforced improvement	Cultivate the importance of improvement. Identifying and solving problems or improving the status needs to be rewarded.
Master scheduling	Consider capacity and flow. Inputs and outputs need to be monitored and capacity organised to optimise flexibility.
Inventory management	Look to minimise inventory, work in progress (WIP) and buffer stocks. Inventory costs money. Look to stock turnovers and hold the minimum that you can to cope with demand.
Pull and synchronisation	This is about flow, look to optimise the whole process not individual parts and make only what is required when it is required.
Measurement	Four key areas for measurement are waste, costs, time and delivery. You need to be able to see improvements or if things are starting to go wrong. Early indicators enable minimal waste further down the line.

48

Learning Styles

When to use
When a team of people need to communicate more effectively.

What you get
Improved levels of communication.

Time
Depends on quantity of information that needs to be shared. Most learning-styles surveys take about half-an-hour to complete, collating and using the information will be an ongoing process.

Number of people
Depends on how many people are giving information and how many people need to receive the information.

Equipment
Equipment is specific to the content being delivered.

Method
1 Determine the content that you want to teach or communicate to others.
2 Consider the different ways which people learn and receive information. Some people prefer diagrams, others prefer detailed text, some need to understand the bigger picture, and some need to learn from the nuts and bolts up. (To name but a few!) So how can we be all things to all people, and ensure everyone understands? If you are communicating to a small group it is worth at this point carrying out a learning-styles survey. There are quite a few on the market, and it will give you an indication of the spread of learning styles in the group, so you can adapt your communication technique accordingly. If you are working with a large group, the only safe way is to cover most of the options.
3 Break the content into small pieces of information.
4 For each piece of information, consider each of the ways people need to receive information. (This can be based on the learning-styles groupings from the survey or for a quick start, see opposite for some common groupings.)
5 Disseminate the information in a range of different ways as described from the table.
6 If possible get feedback as to the success of the information transfer, and modify approach next time accordingly.

Example
Giving directions to a house (see table below).

Exercise
Use the approach to teach about learning styles to a wide audience.

Preferred learning style	Approach
Pictorial – Information absorbed better using pictures.	Draw a map.
Sequential – Information needs to be built up one step at a time.	Explain the route a step at a time from door to door.
Context – bigger picture – Information needs to be seen as part of a larger goal.	You are heading north in the direction of Birmingham.
Simple overview – Information needs to be simple and to the point.	M40 to J9. Turn right, and second right, fourth on left.
Detail to backup – Large levels of detail are required to enable understanding.	Come off the M40 at J9, the one with the hotel at it, on the left you will see a pub, carry on along that road . . .
Auditory or verbal – Understanding requires verbal explanation.	Talk them in on a mobile phone.

Key points

People absorb information in different ways; it is easier to provide information in the style they readily accept rather than force them to learn in a way that isn't natural.

A clash of learning styles can often lead to conflict, it helps if both parties work at presenting their information in a way that the other can easily interpret.

Additional comments

There are many different behavioural tools, methods and questionnaires on the market, all with various merits, which help to improve communication and teamwork. This tool provides a combination of some of the key styles that are recognised.

Learning styles helps you to get the information across to a wide range of people; it does not alter the quality of the information.

Personality profiles can also provide a good indication of how people like to learn.

Other information

There are many books on the area including: G. Dryden and J. Vos, *The Learning Revolution Accelerated Learning Systems*, 1994; R. Riding and S. Rayner, *Cognitive Styles and Learning Strategies*, David Fulton Publishers, 1998.

Prefered learning style	Approach
Pictorial	
Sequential	
Context – bigger picture	
Simple overview	
Detail to backup	
Auditory or verbal	

49

Manufacturing Benchmarks

▓ When to use

To identify potential manufacturing project improvement areas or as part of a manufacturing strategy framework.

▓ What you get

A summary of pre-existent benchmarks in the manufacturing environment which provide useful discussion points when looking for areas for improvement.

▓ Time

A half-day session is usually sufficient.

▓ Number of people

Ideally there will be a multifunctional team, depending on what you hope to gain. As a minimum, have people from manufacturing and representatives from the departments with whom they frequently interact (sales, design, etc.).

▓ Equipment

Copies of the benchmarks for everyone and a means of recording feedback.

▓ Method

There are many manufacturing

> *You need honest and objective input for the process to work.*

benchmarks and internal company standards. This method outlines a generic approach for a typical benchmark.

1 Choose the benchmarks you want to use.
2 Explain what the session is trying to achieve and establish the rules. Tool 4: Brainstorming may help here.
3 Take a point from the benchmark and discuss it with the group.
4 Decide your company matches the description, is better, worse, etc.
5 Repeat steps 2–4 for the rest of the points in the benchmark.
6 Discuss and summarise the main points from the activity. Identify the areas where your company suffers most in comparison to the benchmark.

7 Agree a list of actions to address the main points from the exercise. Tool 26: Effort Impact Graph might help here.

▓ Key points

If your company does not have its own internal benchmarks and you have not completed a recent benchmarking activity as described in Tool 3: Benchmarking, then you can use the benchmarks shown opposite. These are:

● The first table shows the characteristics of a *typical* company from the days of craft through to modern manufacturing. The 'Modern' column should describe your company.
● Doll and Vonderembse's characteristics describe some of the attributes of a modern successful business. Does it describe yours?
● Kim's key tasks ask a number of questions designed to make you think about the important issues for modern manufacturing.
● Hayes and Wheelright describe four evolutionary stages. Stage 4 is the most advanced. At which stage is your company?

▓ Additional comments

Compare your company to the benchmark using a simple scoring system. This helps identify areas for greatest improvement.

When identifying areas for improvement keep in mind the existing business priorities.

As with all benchmarking, seek outside opinion or marketing information to get a more realistic picture of the company's performance.

▓ Other information

Details on each benchmark are in C. Morton, *Becoming World Class*, Macmillan, 1994; W. J. Doll, and M. A. Vonderembse, *Manufacturing Strategy: Process and Content*, Chapman & Hall, 1992; Jay Kim, 'Manufacturing Strategy', an essay in *Financial Times Handbook of Management – Concise Edition* edited by Stuart Crainer; R. H. Hayes and S. C. Wheelright, *Restoring our Competitive Edge: Competing through Manufacturing*, Wiley, 1984; W. Skinner, *Manufacturing: The Formidable Competitive Weapon*, Wiley, 1985; also see Tools 3: Benchmarking; 65: Product – Market Analysis; and 82: Strategy Framework.

Some example benchmarks

(a) Historical stage of development

		Craft	Mass production	Modern
Characteristics	Workers	High skill, involvement, influence and respect.	Low skill, little involvement or respect. Considered as 'just another cog in the machine'.	Intellectual, problem solver, regular training and respect. Contributes to company planning and development.
	Managers	Chaotic, little control, reliance on workers' ability and honesty	Ordered, total control of business operations. Aim for predictability and stability.	Coach and facilitator to co operate with workforce. Thrive on uncertainty and meeting customer needs.
	Customers	High choice but high price with variable quality and delivery.	Lower price with more consistent quality and delivery but limited choice.	High choice, quality and service with low cost. Increasingly high expectations.

(b) Doll und Vonderembse's characteristics

1 Employees appreciate what their internal and external customers want from the business.

2 People throughout the organisation are involved in the decision-making process.

3 Effective communication is encouraged between employees, suppliers and customers with a view to identifying areas for personal and business development.

4 The organisation has a culture that encourages continual and rapid improvement in all areas of the business.

5 Manufacturing increases its flexibility to exploit market uncertainty for competitive advantage.

(c) Jay S. Kim's key tasks of manufacturing

1 *Customer focus* – have you found out what customers want and understood their needs?

2 *Responsibilities* – have you considered how your role integrates with the rest of the supply chain, in particular, order fulfilment and distribution?

3 *Global issues* – is your production global? Can new products be released simultaneously to manufacturing around the world?

4 *Flexibility and rapid response* – are your systems designed to enable rapid changes in product design and demand? Is change viewed as a burden to manufacturing or something that you excel at?

5 *No trade-offs* – are you striving to improve costs, quality, service, flexibility and value or do you still believe that improvements in one will be to the detriment of another?

6 *Culture* – do you encourage an environment of creativity where new challenges motivate the workforce or do you strive to maintain the status quo?

7 *Business links* – do you understand the broader business issues and see where your role fits in and contributes?

(d) Hayes and Wheelright development stages

1 *Internally neutral* – The emphasis is on minimising manufacturing's draining effect on the rest of the business. Performance is measured against manufacturing's own inward looking targets.

2 *Externally neutral* – The goal is to catch up with and follow the main competitors. Spending large amounts of money on one-off projects is seen as the best way to regain competitiveness.

3 *Internally supportive* – Manufacturing provides real support to the corporate strategy. Investments are managed to support systematic long-term improvement strategies.

4 *Externally supportive* – Manufacturing is involved in developing corporate strategy and manufacturing is seen as a means of attaining competitive advantage. Long-term projects aim to acquire capabilities proactively.

50

Marketing Mix

When to use

As part of a product review or while developing a marketing strategy. Also as part of a corporate strategy review.

What you get

A definition of what your company will offer to the market.

Time

Covering the topic in sufficient detail is likely to take about a day of group work plus a few days to research and gather appropriate information.

Number of people

A team of around six, ideally comprising representatives from sales, marketing and finance. It is also useful to include people from design, production and customer support during the 'Product' review stage.

Equipment

Copies of appropriate market, financial and product information for everyone (see below for what is appropriate), a wipe board to capture ideas.

Method

1 Explain the purpose of the session, i.e. either to review the existing product marketing strategy or to develop a strategy for a new product.

2 Review and discuss each of the four 'Ps':
   ● *Product* – including customer benefits, branding, packaging, styling, functionality, characteristics, after-sales support, delivery and installation.
   ● *Price* – including upper limits, lower limits, average market price, profits, perceptions of links between quality and price, effects on company image and other products, special offers, supply and demand relationships.
   ● *Place* – including distribution channels, direct, wholesale or retail, profit margins in the distribution chain, power of

Don't do all of these; do what's right for you and your customers.

distributors, service levels for consumers, feedback from consumers, market segmentation and customer profiles.
   ● *Promotion* – including advertising, brochures, mailshots, sales advisors, promotions, sponsorship, after-sales, timing, budgets and measuring effectiveness.

3 Develop a marketing plan outlining what you will do under each of the four 'Ps'. This represents your offer to the market.

4 Usually additional information will be needed to review and compare the options discussed. Team members should be appointed to gather this information and summarise it.

5 The group should reconvene, discuss any new information and then finalise the marketing plan for implementation.

Example

An outline of the four 'Ps' for a book such as this might look something like this.

Product	Price
An easy-to-use comprehensive management book from a reputable publisher written by qualified authors in a no-nonsense style.	Must be affordable but sensibly priced to reflect the value of the content and comparable to other books in the range.

Place	Promotion
Traditional and specialist bookshops, plus ecommerce and some direct sales. Customers likely to be practising managers and business course students.	University contacts, sales reps to shops, adverts in the specialist press, links to other books in the series, launch at start of the academic year.

Exercise

Review the four 'Ps', then highlight the most important issues for a luxury perfume.

Key points

This technique, like many strategy tools, is not clever in itself, it is merely a checklist. However, because it forces you to be thorough and logical, it improves your chances of developing a sensible plan and reduces the possibility of overlooking something significant.

It also provides you with a valuable internal communication tool.

There is a danger that your company can become too inward looking and lose touch with what the final customer or consumer really wants. Seek outside input or commission a customer survey to bring your views up to date.

■ **Other information**
For an introduction to marketing see P. Doyle, *Marketing Management and Strategy*, Pearson Education, 1997.

Product	Price

Place	Promotion

51

Measurement and Accountability

When to use
When reviewing the organisational structure.

What you get
An understanding of the accountability structure of an organisation.

Time
2 hours will normally provide a useful insight.

Number of people
5–15 people from different areas in the business will give the best results. Although larger groups can be split into smaller syndicate groups to do the exercise.

Equipment
A large area to write on either wipe board or paper on the wall. Five different coloured Post-it™ note packs, enough for about 20 pieces of each colour per person involved.

Method
1 Give each person or syndicate a supply of Post-it™ notes of five different colours. List the things that must be measured in the business/process under evaluation and classify them under headings of *Quality*, *Quantity*, *Time*, *Cost*, or a mixed group of measures which cannot be put into any one of the above categories. Write each one on a colour-coded piece of paper (e.g. red for

Quality, etc.). There must be only one measure per piece of paper. (Allow 20 minutes.)

2 Create the matrix board of Quality, Quantity, etc. on the x-axis and company job titles relevant to the process on the y-axis. (See below.)

3 Place each measurable on the grid relevant to the *Person that will take 'Change Action' because of the meaning of the data* (not just pass it on). Each measure must only appear on one square. (Allow 30 minutes.)

4 Discuss the 'fall out' measures that were difficult to locate. Why should that data be collected anyway? Should any job that has no Post-its™ of a particular colour exist?

5 Define the 'power' structure required and the 'real' measures needed. See Tools 2: Balanced Scorecard or 35: Forward Measurement for additional help here.

Example
See below.

Exercise
Go through the exercise for your family.

Key points
It is important that the exercise is carried out honestly. What actually happens, not what should happen needs to be captured.

Many of the people's roles will be involved in the measures and subsequent actions, but the measure must lie with the first person that does something about it.

Remember, you only get what you measure if the information is acted upon.

ROLE	QUALITY	QUANTITY	TIME	COST	OTHERS
Customer					
CEO				Budget	
Function head				Product cost	
Project head					
Shop supervisor		No. of products			
Scheduler			Schedule compliance		
Worker	Product size				

Additional comments

Do not use this tool as a start point for blaming people. It should be used as a start point for improvement.

Other information

Source: David Alexander, University of Warwick.

ROLE	QUALITY	QUANTITY	TIME	COST	OTHERS

52

Measurement Guidelines

■ When to use
Whenever you need to develop appropriate measurement systems.

■ What you get
Guidance on developing a suitable measurement system.

■ Time
To work through the stages takes about an hour. More time might be needed for more complex situations. It can also be useful to allow a period of reflection between sessions before stage 5.

■ Number of people
Can be performed by an individual. It is more useful if some of the people affected by the new measure to give their input.

■ Equipment
A wipe board to capture ideas, a diagram of the process being measured, existing data to compare ideas.

■ Method
1 Why measure? Establish the reason for developing a new measure. What is it that the organisation hopes to achieve from using this measure?

2 What to measure? Brainstorm all of the factors that could be measured. *Do this if nothing else!* Think about these in terms of the three main measurement options shown on the table opposite.

3 How to measure? Select the options from stage 2 and develop a method by thinking about:
- How should the results be displayed?
- What accuracy/precision is necessary?
- Will measuring the process affect the process?
- Is the measurement system robust enough for the task or subject to external influences?
- Are we making valid assumptions?

4 Select suitable approaches: each of the options from stage 3 should be reviewed in terms of the accuracy, precision, cost, practicality etc. that can be expected. A decision table (Tool 23) may help decide which of the methods is most suitable.

5 Play devil's advocate: brainstorm what people might do to achieve good measures from the measurement system. Are these behaviours likely to help achieve the objectives outlined in stage 1? If not, go back to stage 3.

6 Implement: ensure that the people who are operating the measurement system and those that will use the data it produces are trained.

7 Review and calibration: any measurement system should be periodically reviewed to ensure that it is still operating as intended and that any assumptions made are still valid.

■ Exercise
Develop and evaluate some measures to assess the value you are gaining from this book.

■ Key points
Don't measure just for the sake of it. Successful measurement isn't about the data, it's about what happens as a result of collecting the data.

■ Additional comments
Changes to the product, process, customer requirements and your people can all affect the measurement system – review and change it to keep it appropriate.

■ Other information
See also Tools 35: Forward Measurement, 84: Systems Thinking and 78: Solution Effect Analysis.

	Direct measurement	**Relationship measurement**	**Statistical measurement**
Outline	Comparing something to a known standard, e.g. an object's length on a ruler.	Measuring one factor that is then used to infer another, e.g. measuring the height of mercury to infer temperature.	Measuring a few items in a batch then using statistics to make predictions about all of the other items.
Examples	Length, height, lead-time, sales growth, returns on investment.	Temperature, structural strain, production costing, sales forecasts.	Quality sampling, process control, trend analysis, customer surveys.
Accuracy	Determined by calibration and sufficient readings.	Determined by calibration, sufficient readings, resistance of the relationship to outside influences, and consistency of the relationship over the range of measurements taken.	Determined by calibration, sufficient readings, together with an understanding of the statistics and the environment that they are being used in.
Precision	Determined by the user's ability and the standards being measured against.	Determined by the user's ability, the standards being measured against and the strength of the relationship.	Determined by the statistical nature of the system.
Advantages	It is simple to understand and use the results, quick to obtain readings, usually cheap to perform and training the user is normally simple	It can measure factors that may be impractical to measure directly. Many relationships can produce high precision and accuracy while still being simple to use and understand	Can significantly reduce the number of readings (hence time and cost) needed. Can be used where it may be impractical to use direct or relationship measurement. Can be used to identify unusual trends and help prevent errors. Is less sensitive to operator error.
Disadvantages	Its use can be limited by the practicality of obtaining direct comparisons. It may be time consuming and costly to obtain a large number of readings. It can be sensitive to user error.	May be time consuming and costly to obtain a large number of readings. Can be sensitive to user error. Suitable relationships do not always exist. Misplaced confidence may be afforded to measurements without understanding the limitations of the relationship and its effect on precision and accuracy.	May be time consuming and costly to produce the initial statistical information. May be difficult to update the statistics in a fast-changing environment. Methods employed may be difficult to understand and so be interpreted or used incorrectly. Relies on the system being statistically stable and predictable.
Summary	A simple and quick measurement system that can be accurate and precise. Unfortunately, it is not always practical to use.	Relatively simple and quick measurement system that can be accurate and precise. Unfortunately it is not always practical to use. The user needs to understand the nature and limitations of the relationship used.	Relatively cheap and reliable alternative in most high-volume stable environments. Like all measurement systems, it needs to be calibrated and maintained for optimum results. The principles of the system understood by anyone who is using its results.

53

Meeting Management

■ When to use
Whenever you have the responsibility for chairing a meeting. It is particularly useful for virtual meetings such as audio or video conferencing.

■ What you get
Better time management, outcomes more likely to meet the meeting objectives.

■ Time
Ideally meetings last half-an-hour to 2 hours. Although meetings can take longer the effectiveness of the meeting will reduce beyond this time.

■ Number of people
The fewer the better. Only those with unique knowledge, contribution or whose buy-in will be needed for the effective implementation of any ideas.

■ Equipment
An agenda that details those items that are necessary and sufficient to achieve the meeting's objective. Also have a clear definition of venue, start time and time allocated to the meeting.

■ Method
1 The following points are fundamental to managing an effective meeting if you are the nominated 'Chair'.
2 Have a clear unambiguous objective for the meeting. If this were achieved in the time allocated the meeting would be regarded as a success.
3 Define the agenda. Include only those items that are necessary and sufficient to meet the objective.
4 Notionally allocate time to each item and nominate one of the attendees to address them. This will require their prior agreement.
5 Publish the agenda in good time and follow up with each person responsible for an agenda item.

6 If there are different issues to address, make sure that you have a thorough discussion prior to the meeting with those attending the meeting who are likely to have difficulty or objection to a particular course of action.
7 Be there early and start the meeting on time to show your commitment to time management.
8 State the objective and time planned for the meeting. Make it clear that the success of the meeting depends on achieving this objective within the timeframe.
9 You must allow a full discussion relevant to the achievement of the objective. However, you must focus the discussion on facts relevant to the achievement of the objective, not rhetoric or trying to change history. Any outspoken people who ramble or divert from the purpose must be asked 'How does this contribute to the objective?' Be strong at controlling non-focused or non-constructive discussion.
10 Take particular note of people who have said little or have not contributed at all. After each topic encourage them to make an input.
11 Most of all, remember the 'power of the pen' (POTP), and volunteer that you or your nominated secretary will write up the actions from the meeting. Take particular note of what was agreed or not agreed on each agenda item and summarise it during the meeting, together with those who are actioned before moving onto the next item on the agenda.

■ Exercise
Use the process highlighted above for your next meeting.

■ Additional comments
Where you are not the nominated 'Chair', there are two possible courses of action.

1 If there is a nominated 'Chair'; agree with them the objective and agenda. Volunteer to write this down. Remember the POTP. Also volunteer to address the items most likely to secure your desired outcome.

2   If there is no nominated 'Chair', prepare a draft objective for the meeting together with an agenda and have a discussion with as many attendees as you can to secure their agreement to it prior to the meeting. Remember once again the POTP.

Many software packages have standard templates for meeting agendas and minutes, which can be very useful. Below is an example of an agenda template.

An interesting technique used to discourage time wasting during meetings was to show the running cost of the meeting. The Chair entered a notional salary of everyone present into a laptop program, which then displayed the combined cost/minute as the meeting progressed.

Meeting Management – Example Agenda

Meeting objective:
Date:
Venue:
Start time:
Finish time:
Attendees:

Meeting items	Person responsible	Time allocated	Outcome/ Actions
1.			

54

Networking

When to use

When you want a group of people to learn about the principles behind good networking.

What you get

A realisation that you already have a powerful network. Also, some actions to effectively use networking on an ongoing basis.

Time

To do the exercise will take about half-an-hour. Developing the action plan to make use of the potential revealed from strategic networking will take 2–4 hours.

Number of people

14–30 is ideal, providing enough people to make it realistic yet few enough for it not to get out of control.

Equipment

A list of living famous people's names from a variety of backgrounds relevant to the group, e.g. pop stars, actors, political figures, sports personalities, etc.

Method

1 Set the exercise up as a challenge. In groups of three or four, the challenge is to use your team's existing network to gain access to the famous people on the list. Allow 20 minutes for this.

2 Review who managed to make connections to which famous people, count the number of people they had to contact to get to them and the nature of the route.

3 Consider the fact that, if these are the results that you get without really trying, what would be possible if as a team we worked at networking?

4 Develop ideas and actions to strategically maximise the potential network that is available to the business.

Example

Actions resulting from running the exercise:

● Attend more industry functions and general business events, focus on meeting and engaging with people. Learn how to circulate at such events.
● Create a system to enable easier connection making.
● Enrol on some 'active listening' courses.
● Actively promote the achievements of others in our network.
● Actively set out to meet some people and review in two months' time.
● Understand who the really good networkers in the company are, and share their advice on networking.
● Make a point of getting back in touch with people that you haven't spoken to for a while.
● Put different parts of the network in touch with each other.

Exercise

Network to get a conversation with the chairperson of the residents association in your local area.

Key points

Trust me! Normally the majority of the famous people are accessed via three to six connections.

This tool provides an awareness of the opportunity that exists in terms of networking, the real benefits come when you begin to really work the network.

You don't need to know every one, if you ask the right questions you can normally get to who you want to through other people.

Additional comments

Some people may be a little wary of the subject of networking, it is important to understand that networking doesn't have to be the showering of business cards, the false show conversations and using another person for your own gain. Good networking is about building relationships at a much deeper level.

The giving and receiving of help, advice and knowledge.

Effective networking is about building a high trust reputation with those who you meet (and have yet to meet), it is about becoming someone who is worth knowing.

■ **Other information**

Source: Roy Sheppard. For further information on Networking, see www.RoySpeaks.com, and R. Sheppard, *Rapid Result Referrals*, Centre Publishing, 2001.

Guidelines

- **Do not contact others only when you want something – people notice.**

- **Be proactive about making matches between the skills and knowledge of the people you meet and put them in touch with those you have already established a relationship with.**

- **Identify gaps in your network. Work to fill them.**

- **Consider who in your network are givers and who are takers. Some people are takers – realise this and avoid where possible. 'Give to givers'.**

- **Get past surface relationships by learning more about what makes them tick, their family or educational background. Be respectful of everyone you meet.**

- **Don't let people down.**

- **Make it a priority to get to know all sorts of people within the company.**

- **Consider what you could do to help those around you achieve what they are striving for.**

- **Think about who would find particular information valuable, as long as it isn't confidential – share it. Proactively trade information and knowledge. Be valuable to others.**

- **Attend seminars and conferences, get a delegate list beforehand and formulate a plan to target people.**

Used with permission from *Rapid Result Referrals* by Roy Sheppard.

55

Optimised Production Technology (OPT)

When to use
When looking to improve a production facility in terms of increased throughput, reduced inventory and operating expense. Particularly effective in high volume, mechanical assembly type industries.

What you get
An idea of where the bottlenecks are and priorities for increasing throughput and removing inventory.

Time
This is an ongoing process, and way of working.

Number of people
Needs to involve everyone who is a stakeholder in the part of the business in which it is being introduced. It will require an extensive educational process through all levels and all departments.

Equipment
The software to support the philosophy is optional.

Method
1 OPT uses three measures: *Throughput* – the rate that the system generates money, i.e. when it's sold. *Inventory* – all the money that the system has invested in purchasing things that it intends to sell. *Operating expense* – all the system spends in order to turn inventory into throughput.
2 There are nine rules of OPT which are shown opposite with a brief description of each.
3 Initially OPT needs to be understood by the company's management, and its applicability to their particular organisation needs to be analysed and discussed.

4 Only when the concept is bought into can a pilot project be designed and run. The understanding of the measures and the nine rules will provide a basis for its implementation. Once running changes can be implemented to refine the system specific to the company's requirements. It can then be rolled out through the entire plant.

Example
Walking with a group of people up a mountain. The aim is to get everyone to the top together and safely.

The time taken to complete the mission (throughput) is determined by the slowest person (the bottleneck). Having some of the party speed off to the top of the mountain on their own does not improve throughput, but increases the risks of things going wrong. Ideally everyone walks up the mountain at the same pace thus encouraging the slower people and maintaining safety.

Exercise
Consider the implications of OPT for making a cup of tea.

Key points
Education and training is key. Its successful introduction may require external support.

Many companies have successfully employed the OPT philosophy without the software. However, rules 7, 8 and 9 are very complicated to introduce without software.

OPT does not work well in job shops and is largely untried in fast process industries.

It is important to consider the implications of OPT on existing systems. Many of the conventional rules of production planning are challenged by OPT, therefore its introduction needs to be thorough as it will challenge the way people have worked for years.

■ Additional comments

OPT is not a magic answer.

A major obstacle to the introduction of OPT is that applying the rules, scheduling and philosophy it advocates would push the manufacturer towards poor performance against existing measures, e.g. capacity utilisation. This is compensated for by the introduction of the alternative measurement system. This can be received cynically, as there is no firm baseline from which to determine if the benefits are real or a trick of the books. Therefore the first real barrier to overcome is the acceptance of the new measures.

■ Other information

The original concept and best book on the subject is E. Goldratt and J. Cox, *The Goal – Beating the Competition*, Creative Output Books, 1986. Other books on the subject are K. Johnson, *Implementing Optimised Production Technology*, IFS, 1990 and G. Jones and M. Roberts, *Optimised Production Technology*, IFS, 1990.

Rules for Optimised Production Technology

Rule	Description
1. Balance flow not capacity	Balancing the flow enables a steady 'drum beat' to be established which enables WIP to be kept low due to the stability it creates.
2. The level of utilisation of a non-bottleneck is not determined by its own potential but some other constraint in the system.	The only machine or workstation which should be working at 100% is the bottleneck, all other non-bottlenecks should be working at a rate to ensure that the bottleneck maximises utilisation of the critical resource.
3. Utilisation and activation of a resource are not synonymous.	Idle material is viewed as a crime. Material that is not being used is considered as waste.
4. An hour lost at a bottleneck is an hour lost for the whole system.	The bottleneck determines the flow of work through the system. Losing time at the bottleneck will reduce flow through the system. Likewise, if you save time at a bottleneck you increase the flow rate.
5. An hour saved at a non-bottleneck is just a mirage.	Any time saved at a non-bottleneck will merely contribute to idle time and not add to throughput.
6. Bottlenecks govern both throughput and inventories.	The bottleneck is the governing factor on throughput. Inventory at non-bottlenecks should be kept at a level to ensure optimum productivity at the bottleneck.
7. The transfer batch may not, and in many times should not, be equal to the process batch.	Transfer batch: quantity that activates operation. Process batch: balances inventory cost, set-up cost, etc. to provide flexibility. Transfer batch is appropriate size from the standpoint of the 'part'. Process batch is appropriate size from the standpoint of resource.
8. The process batch should be variable not fixed.	Ideally large process batches at bottlenecks and small process batches at non-bottlenecks.
9. Schedules should be established by looking at all of the constraints simultaneously. Lead times are the result of a schedule and cannot be predetermined.	Analyse the process to identify all likely bottlenecks, then schedule for these resources-based priorities and available capacity.

56

Option Generation – TOWS (Threats, Opportunities, Weaknesses, and Strengths)

When to use
When you need to be creative in selecting ways forward but prefer to think logically.

What you get
A list of possible actions based on a company's strengths, weaknesses, opportunities, and threats.

Time
A SWOT analysis needs to be completed first. A quick TOWS can be completed in about 45 minutes. Working methodically through every possibility (see below) can take much longer.

Number of people
From one to many although, for practicality, 2–10 is most useful.

Equipment
A large wipe board to record results.

Method
1 Complete a SWOT analysis (Tool 83) for the issue being investigated.

To reduce the number of possible combinations, try grouping the individual SWOT items into major groups.

2 Summarise the main outputs from the SWOT on a chart as shown in the example.
3 Work through the chart by comparing pairs of statements. For example take the first strength and compare it to the first opportunity. See if the group can generate an idea to address or exploit the combination.
4 Repeat this process for all combinations.

Example
The table opposite is a TOWS analysis for the idea of producing this book.

Exercise
Complete a TOWS grid for any SWOT you might have previously completed. If you have not done a SWOT before, do one for yourself personally in your job. Use this to complete a TOWS grid to identify training or career opportunities.

Key points
The aim is to help logical thinkers to create a large number of possible actions using a systematic approach.

To be thorough every possible combination on the grid can be considered. However, in practice, a good facilitator can quickly home in on the areas that are creating the most ideas.

It is not necessary to try to grade the value of the ideas at this stage. It is more important to create many options, which can be evaluated later.

You can add two extra boxes to compare strengths and weaknesses and opportunities and threats.

Additional comments
It can be dangerous to make decisions based on unrealistic information and many companies have a biased view of their own situation. To avoid problems try gaining input from impartial or external sources.

This tool can be used at a number of different levels from individual to company strategy.

There are a number of alternatives for completing the grid. Firstly, it is not always advisable to work through the combinations systematically. Some people prefer to be able to tackle combinations in a more freeform order. Secondly, while brainstorming solutions in a group can be useful for quick results, it can become less efficient for larger projects. Instead, it can be beneficial to let the team complete the grid in their own time. A follow-up meeting can then be held to review and discuss everyone's ideas.

	Strengths – Know lots of tools – Practical experience – Know how to teach tools	**Weaknesses** – No publishing experience – No facilities to publish
Opportunities – People want a tool book – There are no simple-to-use cover-all books	Talk to people about what they want then write a book	Work with an experienced publisher for this market
Threats – Someone might write one before us – Conflicts with our main business	Use the book to promote our activities	Register with a publisher ASAP

	Strengths	**Weaknesses**
Opportunities	What options are apparent when putting together strengths and opportunities?	What options are apparent when putting together weaknesses and opportunities?
Threats	What options are apparent when putting together strengths and threats?	What options are apparent when putting together weaknesses and threats?

57

Order Qualifiers and Order Winners

When to use
When considering which areas to focus on for improvement.

What you get
A customer-focused view of areas of importance to your business.

Time
Depends on how it is run, as there are two options. You can either invite a selection of customers to the session in which case it will take about half a day of their time and then require a review and action session. Alternatively you can have three separate sessions. (1) a 2-hour initial design of template; (2) time set aside to do research; (3) a 2–4 hour review and action stage.

Number of people
The research ideally needs to be done with a selection of key customers and potential customers (these can be internal or external). For the analysis ideally you need from your business a selection of the people who can make decisions as to the future direction. More than 20 in total is not advised.

Equipment
Visible display and somewhere to capture developments.

Method
1 Begin the session by explaining what order qualifiers (OQ) and order winners (OW) are:
   Order qualifiers: elements of customer requirements that are the bare minimum without which they would not even consider the offer.
   Order winners: elements of customer requirements, which are the ones that sway the decision on who to go with.
2 Brainstorm OQ and OW for your business (or part of the business). Narrow the list down to between 15 and 20 for each and develop a review sheet as shown opposite.

3 Carry out research to identify which of the order qualifiers and winners the customers require and where you sit in term of providing them.
4 Review the findings in terms of the customer needs and your current performance, looking specifically at areas where there are inconsistencies between requirement and provision.

> You could also get the customers to rank them, to provide further information.

5 Determine areas for focus in the future, agree actions, and set up a review process.

Example
For this book:

Order Qualifiers	C	U	Order Winners	C	U
Knowledge	✓	✓	Easy to use	✓	✓
Something new	✓	✓	Hardback	✓	
Main tools	✓	✓	1 tool per page		✓
Useful	✓	✓	On shelf October	✓	✓
<100 pages	✓		Reasonable price	✓	✓
Credible		✓	Others recommend it.	✓	✓

C = Customer, U = Us

In this case, the areas for immediate focus would be the possibility of reducing it to less than 100 pages, followed by the option of it being made in hardback. Finally, consider the removal of the constraint of one page per tool as this is something that the customer doesn't feel strongly about.

Exercise
Complete a qualifier, winner analysis for purchasing a television.

Key points
Make sure you look at key customers – be careful of getting misdirected by the requests of just one obscure customer.

It can be used at many levels in organisations from individual to whole business.

■ Additional comments

This tool highlights the gaps, not the solutions on how to fill them. It is important that it is used as a start point for further research into costs of development and potential returns, etc.

It is possible to add an extra column to the grid to plot what key competitors offer, enabling you to focus on areas for differentiation. It can also be useful to use a scoring system and mark your performance on a scale of 1–10.

■ Other information

T. Hill develops and explains the concept of order qualifiers and winners in his book, *Manufacturing Strategy*, Macmillan, 1985, and N. Slack combines it with the implications for manufacturing focus in *The Manufacturing Advantage*, Mercury Books, 1991. See also Tool 82: Strategy Framework for a further development of this tool.

ORDER QUALIFIERS	CUSTOMER	US	ORDER WINNERS	CUSTOMER	US

58

Pie Diagrams

When to use
When needing to display information in a simple, high impact manner.

What you get
A visible representation of data.

Time
Assuming all of the data is already collected, 10–30 minutes.

Number of people
One person is required to develop the chart. Its usefulness is in its display and discussion with others.

Equipment
Paper or computer to develop the chart. Many computer programs create pie charts automatically.

Method
1. Put the data into a table.
2. Calculate the percentage of the total for each of the categories. This is done by dividing the amount for the category by the total amount and multiplying it by 100.
3. Draw a circle on a piece of paper; the entire circle represents 100%.
4. Mark off each of the categories on the circle as to their respective percentage of the whole and ensure they are clearly labelled. Continue until the circle is fully labelled.

Example
Flight sample from an airport.

Flight status	Number	Percentage (%)
On time	70	91
Delayed	5	6
Cancelled	2	3
Total	**77**	**100**

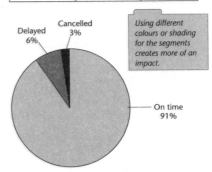

Using different colours or shading for the segments creates more of an impact.

Quite clearly from the diagram it is possible to see that most of the flights were on time. It could also instigate the need for further research into why such a large percentage were delayed or cancelled.

Exercise
Create a pie chart for the following information about the hair colour of students in a class.

Light brown – 12
Blonde – 3
Red – 1
Dark brown – 15

Key points
The pie chart clearly identifies the largest shares of the data.

Pie charts are very useful as they are often used and seen in everyday life, therefore people are used to seeing and understanding them.

Be clear to mark each of the segments in terms of their subject and percentage.

Additional comments
This is a very simple means of displaying information. It does not provide any explanation or reasoning behind the chart. The chart is only really useful for data that is easily categorised.

Category	Number	Percentage (%)
Total		100

59

Power Maps

When to use
When wanting to understand whom the key influencers in an organisation are. Particularly useful in a sales environment.

What you get
A picture of the power structure of a group of people.

Time
1–2 hours to develop the map.

Number of people
Ideally a group of 2–5, to develop the map. It can be done alone, however, it is likely to provide a fairly biased analysis.

Equipment
A wipe board or flipchart to capture the output of the session.

Method
1 Agree on and gain a common understanding of the context that the group of people are to be studied under, e.g. subject area, project team. Summarise the context into a short sentence.
2 Determine all of the people who are involved.
3 Arrange the people's names in a circle on the flipchart or wipe board. Ensure you leave plenty of space between the names for adding arrows later.
4 Look for cause/influence relationships between each of the people and connect them with arrows. If there is no influence relationship between the people, do not put in an arrow. If there is a relationship the point of the arrow needs to go to the factor that is most influenced (not the one that influences). *Do not draw two-headed arrows.* Base your decisions on the relationship on the behaviours you have seen and experienced.
5 Check that the diagram is complete and accurate.

6 Tally the number of ingoing and outgoing arrows for each person.
7 Redraw the diagram including the number of ingoing and outgoing arrows for each person. Highlight the person that has the *most outgoings* as the likely *key influencer* in the context.
8 Initially focus on the key influencer; this is likely to be your point of maximum leverage in the context.

Example
See opposite.

Exercise
Power map a group of children when given the suggestion of a new game.

Key points
The map which is developed is likely to be fairly sensitive as it could be construed as manipulative. Be sensitive to where it is kept and how it is used.

This tool can also be used by identifying the final decision maker and focusing on the people who have direct arrows going into that person, to maximise the chance of the decision going your way.

The session needs to be carefully facilitated to prevent it becoming a 'talking or gossip shop'. Different situations/contexts reveal different power maps even for the same group of people. The key influencer is normally the one, which if focused on will have the greatest impact on the outcome. This is not based on organisational structure; it is to do with real influences.

For a more refined approach it is possible to put a weighting on the arrows to indicate the strength of influence. This significantly increases the complexity of the tool.

The methodology behind power maps can also be used to understand the influence relationships in between different factors surrounding an issue. See Tool 43: Influence Diagrams.

▪ Additional comments

The diagrams often become over complicated and impossible to decipher. To minimise the risk of this work with a maximum of 20 people and only indicate major influences.

This tool does not provide you with a solution; it points you to the area of most leverage. Although it provides an outcome that is fairly subjective, it is useful.

It is important not to concentrate exclusively on the key influencer because the aggregate influence of the others may be significant. See also Tool 54: Networking.

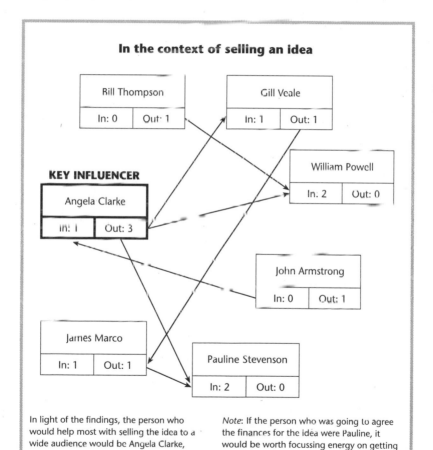

In light of the findings, the person who would help most with selling the idea to a wide audience would be Angela Clarke, therefore it would be beneficial to ensure she is bought into the idea and has a clear understanding of it.

Note: If the person who was going to agree the finances for the idea were Pauline, it would be worth focussing energy on getting James and Angela to buy into the idea (particularly if you don't have access to Pauline directly).

60

Presenting – Communication

When to use
When designing a presentation.

What you get
A rigorous approach to designing a thorough presentation.

Time
Will vary depending on the length and content of the presentation, put aside at least half a day.

Number of people
1–5. Ideally the people who are involved with the information that is being presented.

Equipment
Presentation equipment.

Method
1 Think carefully as to what you want the audience to take from the presentation. Think in terms of key facts, feelings, actions and perceptions. Note these down and create a conclusions side that captures the essence of these key elements.

2 Now think about your audience, who are they, how many, what are their backgrounds, what are their expectations, what interests them, what is important to them. Put yourself into your audience's shoes and understand what would capture their attention. Note these things down and create an introduction slide to capture the audiences' attention.

3 Create a storyboard or a set of panels (see opposite) to take the audience on a journey from the introduction slide through to the conclusions slide.

   It is always worth checking that they understood the message that you were putting across.

4 Develop the presentation using the storyboard for guidance.

5 Check the flow and consistency of the presentation. (It is well worth doing a run through to someone who is fresh to the presentation.)

6 Deliver the presentation.

Example
See opposite for a storyboard on the subject of the importance of exercise.

Exercise
Create a 10-minute presentation on how to create a successful presentation.

Key points
● Keep it simple.
● Say how long you are going to talk for and stick to it.
● Don't try and put too much information on a slide.
● Be careful not to use jargon.
● Think about the learning styles of the audience (see Tool 48: Learning Styles). If you don't know what they are or it is a big group, ensure you use a combination of styles, e.g. diagrams and text.
● Be careful with the use of jokes – they often fall flat in presentations.
● Ensure the level of detail is appropriate.
● It often helps to keep things on track by having the agenda visible at all times.
● Be yourself, and do it your way, it will appear much more congruent that way.

Additional comments
Food for thought: 'Tell them what your going to tell them', then, 'Tell them', then, 'Tell them what you've told them'.

And remember: 'Tell me and I might hear. Show me and I may see. Involve me and I will learn'.

Other information
Useful books on presentation skills are:
A. Bradbury, *Successful Presentation Skills*, Kogan Page, 2000; S. Mandel, *Effective Presentation Skills*, Kogan Page, 1995.

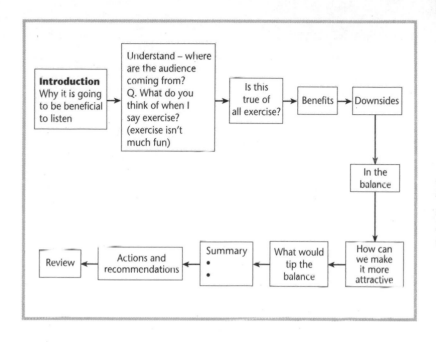

61

Pricing Strategies

When to use
When introducing a new product into a marketplace. Use as part of a business strategy development process.

What you get
A number of pricing strategies, each of which can be modelled to assess the impact on company profitability.

Time
About 1 hour to get an understanding of each of the strategies, and another 1–2 hours to run through each of the strategies and the implications for your business.

Number of people
5–17 people. Ideally from different parts of the business, including finance, marketing, sales and operations.

Equipment
The check sheet shown opposite.

Method
1 Describe each of the pricing strategies, as shown in the table opposite.
2 Complete the chart shown opposite, discussing the implications of each of the strategies to your business and the specific product that is being launched.
3 Decide on an appropriate strategy and create an action plan to take it forward.

Strategy	Description
Market skimming	High price – competing either on uniqueness or quality. Unlikely to be much competition, maintaining this strategy will require additional support from the business such as in branding, etc.
Sliding or reducing skim	Start with a high price, as competitors enter the market gradually reduce the price. This is likely in situations where it is difficult to sustain a technological advantage or where costs are sensitive to economies of scale.
Market penetration	Low price is used to obtain volume sales and to attain market share. The price must not be so low that it indicates poor quality or unacceptable performance.
Floor pricing	Very low price is used to appeal to those who are very price conscious. Enterprises that can survive such low margins can do normally due to high turnover, low overheads or lower profit requirements. Need to closely monitor costs.
Competitor pricing	The price is set relative to a competitor's price; it can be higher or lower depending on the 'competitive advantage' you are selling on.
Cost-based pricing	All of the strategies above imply that costs be managed to produce an adequate profit, in line with the pricing strategy which is adopted. This strategy identifies the costs and determines a price on a cost plus profit basis.

Example

When selling designer clothes, a market skimming strategy would be appropriate, as they will be competing on uniqueness, and targeting a market whose primary purchasing decisions will be on that basis and the price of the item would be of little concern.

Exercise

Consider the pricing strategy that would be the most appropriate for a company wanting to sell parachutes.

Key points

It is difficult and often impossible to raise prices once they have been set.

Consider the implications to the rest of the business, e.g. entering the market with a floor pricing strategy when the brand and the rest of the products are sold on quality and a skimming style of pricing strategy could send confusing signals to customers and ultimately damage the brand.

It is vital that the pricing strategy adopted provides adequate profit as a product in the portfolio. It is also important that the pricing of a new product does not destroy margins on more established products, see Tool 67: Product Life Cycles.

Additional comments

This tool is very linear in nature; in reality there may be a combination of strategies used.

Strategy	Description	Implications
Market skimming	High price – competing either on uniqueness (niche) or quality.	
Sliding or reducing skim	Start with a high price, as competitors enter the market and gradually reduce the price.	
Market penetration	Low price is used to obtain volume sales and to attain market share. May initially be loss making until volumes build up therefore may need to be supported by other products.	
Floor pricing	Very low price is used to appeal to those who are very price conscious. However, must generate profits or projected to when volume targets are met.	
Competitor pricing	The price is set relative to a competitor's price; it can be higher or lower depending on the 'competitive advantage' you are selling on. However, it must not destroy product portfolio profitability.	
Cost-based pricing	This strategy identifies the costs and determines a price on a cost plus profit basis.	

62

Prioritisation Matrix

When to use
When you have a number of actions and you need to determine which need to be done first.

What you get
A helicopter view of the actions and a start point for selecting which in order to approach them.

Time
From 10 minutes to 1 hour depending on the level it is being used at.

Number of people
You can do it in a group or on your own depending on the nature of the task list.

Equipment
Flip chart, wipe board or, if doing it alone, a piece of paper.

Method
1. List all of the tasks you have to do. This could be your personal to do list or a project action list.
2. Draw up the four-box grid as shown in the diagram.
3. Position each of the tasks on the grid in terms of their relative importance and urgency. At this stage, it is often worth checking with someone else the positioning you select, as what might seem most important to you, may not be the most important to your boss.

4. Use the grid to begin to place an order on the tasks in terms of whether they are high or low importance and urgency.

| | IMPORTANT | |
	LOW	HIGH
URGENT HIGH	3. These tend to be the tasks that get done first if you don't take time to consider the relative importance of the activity.	1. Worth doing these first.
URGENT LOW	4. Consider if these are worth doing at all.	2. Do these next, as they often very quickly flip into the category above with little warning.

Example
A 'To do' list.

– Phone Zoë.
– Create workshop packs.
– Print out report.
– Post invoice.
– Phone David.
– Book restaurant.

| | IMPORTANT | |
	LOW	HIGH
URGENT HIGH	Book restaurant	Create workshop packs Post invoice
URGENT LOW	Phone Zoë Phone Dave	Print out report

So the order to carry out would be:
1. Create workshop packs.
2. Post invoice.
3. Print out report.
4. Book restaurant, then if time phone Zoë and Dave.

Exercise
Use the template to prioritise your 'To do' list for today.

Prioritisation Matrix

■ Key points

Urgent is not the same as important.

This is a really useful tool when a lot of fire fighting is going on and you have so much to do you can't see the wood for the trees.

You can use the tool either as a planning tool or for a reflective tool. If using it as a reflective tool, list all of the tasks that you have done and place them on the grid. Next consider the ones you didn't manage to do and highlight them on the grid. Are there any patterns emerging? What could you do to optimise your time?

It can be very useful discussing the positioning with both your boss and colleagues, to check for their perceived positioning. Their involvement will help you to manage your time more effectively and give them an understanding of the scope of the tasks you take on.

■ Additional comments

Beware, don't involve too many people, everyone has different opinions; focus on the ones that are important, not the ones that are loudest.

It is important you don't spend too much time on this as over analysing may end up cutting into the time you need to do the tasks.

Watch out for changing importance and urgency of a task.

IMPORTANT

LOW   HIGH

URGENT

HIGH

LOW

63

Process Control Charts

When to use
To detect/reduce changes in a process, and proactively control the quality (reduce variability) of its output.

What you get
Statistical confidence that a process is under control, or a pre-emptive indication of a process deteriorating.

Time
This is an ongoing process; training will be necessary for the operators using statistical process control (SPC). A chart must be set up for each process or machine.

Number of people
Typically one person per process would be responsible for capturing the data.

Equipment
Calculator and somewhere to capture and display the charts. There is software on the market to support control charts.

Method
1 Select the process to be monitored, and a suitable measure of output quality.
2 Samples of the process output are required at regular intervals.
3 Select a sample size (ideally as large as is possible given time/cost constraints, five is the best compromise statistically).
4 Select a sample period (based on the potential rate of change of the process and cost of sampling versus risk cost of not detecting a process deterioration).
5 Select an appropriate control chart. Many different charts exist depending on type of measurements made and sample size. They all work on the principle of controlling the average and spread (range) of a process output, and are listed in Key points.
6 Take 20 initial samples at the given sample period. Allow some variation about the period to ensure that the samples are random.

7 Calculate the control limits for the process (see example). These are plotted on the chart as bounds against which the process is evaluated. They are commonly set ± 3 standard deviations (s.d.) from the process average (mean).
8 Continue sampling and plot the results on the chart. Look for an out-of-control process (see Key points).

Example
See opposite.

Exercise
Consider the schedule adherence of suppliers to your business. Monitor it to provide indications of actions needed.

Key points

Chart selection
Continuous variable measured, e.g. length:

Moving range – where only one item of data is measured (useful for management data).
Mean and range ($\bar{X}/R$) – most commonly used where sample size is greater than one.
Mean and sigma – used when sample size is greater than 10.

Attribute measured, e.g. number of defects:

Proportion defective – when number in sample varies.
Number of defects – when sample size is constant.

Out-of-control indications
A process is said to be 'out of control' when variations occur which are not natural. This is true if one of the following conditions apply:

● One or more points fall outside of the control limits.
● When the control chart is divided into zones and any of the following are true:

```
------------------------------------ UCL
            Zone A
            Zone B
            Zone C
            Zone C            Average
            Zone B
            Zone A
------------------------------------ LCL
```

  – 2 out of 3 consecutive points are on the same side of the average in Zone A.
  – 4 points out of 5 consecutive points are on the same side of the average in Zone B or beyond.

- 9 consecutive points are on one side of the average.
- 6 consecutive points, increasing or decreasing.
- 14 consecutive points that alternate up and down.
- 15 consecutive points within Zone C either above or below the average.

Watch for progressive changes in the chart, as it could mean that a maintenance check is needed.

■ Other information
Walter Shewhart invented control charts more than 60 years ago. For further information see: J. S. Oakland, *SPC – A Practical Guide*, Heinemann, 1986; also see Tool 76: Six Sigma.

Process Control Charts – Example
We take a continuous measurement every half hour, sample size = 5, and selected a mean and range chart (X/R – the most commonly used).

20 initial samples were taken and the control limits calculated. The sample average ($\bar{X}$) and sample range (R) are calculated using the equations:

$$X = \frac{\text{Sum of the measurements for all outputs in sample}}{\text{number of outputs in sample}}$$

R = Largest measurement − smallest measurement

The control limits are calculated based on ± 3 s.d., but are transformed to the mean range of a set of samples by dividing by d_2. This is because the control chart is based only on the within-sample variance, and not the between-sample variance.

No. of samples (n)	d_2	No. of samples (n)	d_2	No. of samples (n)	d_2
1	1.128	5	2.236	9	2.970
2	1.128	6	2.534	10	3.078
3	1.693	7	2.704	11	3.178
4	2.059	8	2.847	12	3.258

Subsequent samples are plotted below and checked against the out-of-control criteria.

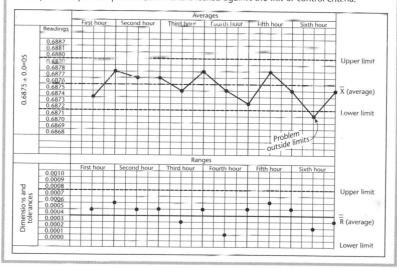

64

Process Mapping – IDEF

When to use
When process mapping a part of or a whole business.

What you get
A consistent graphical representation of how a system or process works.

Time
Depends on the complexity of the process being analysed and the level of detail that is required. Normally takes weeks not days to develop.

Number of people
Ideally involve the people who are responsible for each of the areas to give a realistic view of what goes on (and eventually how it can be improved).

Equipment
Somewhere to capture the process map. (Computer software is available to aid process map development.)

Method
1 Identify the part of the business which is to be mapped – focus on defining the start and finish point.
2 Produce a high-level flowchart, see Tool 31: Flowcharting.
3 Start at one end of the process and break the flowchart down into specific activities and label as shown in the activity diagram opposite. Each activity box represents a process or subprocess and has a detailed description in the glossary. However, to maintain simplicity this will be summarised by one verb in the map.
4 Continue through the process connecting outputs and inputs. (It is possible to have multiple inputs and outputs.)

5 Once having done the high-level map, it is possible to look in further detail at some or all of the parts of the business; these are labelled according to the process number as shown. This enables easy retracing of processes as:
  – A_0 provides context diagram (high-level diagram)
  – A_2 provides more detail on process 2
  – A_{24} provides detail on process 2, subprocess 4

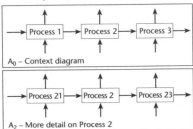

A_0 – Context diagram

A_2 – More detail on Process 2

6 The maps can then be used to highlight areas of waste, problems or opportunities to improve.

Exercise
Create a process map for washing clothes.

Key points
This method's key benefit is that it provides a consistent approach to the development of process maps and thus provides consistent interpretation.

It is important to determine the level of detail that will be useful for you to go to. Producing very detailed maps is time consuming and often provides few benefits. Always keep in mind what you are trying to achieve by the exercise and why.

It enables business processes to be modelled separately to organisational structure.

Keep the number of processes at any one level to fewer than six. Otherwise it gets too complicated to analyse, it will also help to keep the detail at a useful level.

Additional comments
There are many different standards for process mapping, see also Tool 89: Time Based Process Mapping (TBPM). IDEF is often the more recognised approach.

This technique comes from the US Air Force, it was developed primarily to document manufacturing processes although its use now has spread well beyond that area. Also see C. Feldmann, *The Practical Guide to Process Reengineering using IDEF0*, Dorset House, 1998.

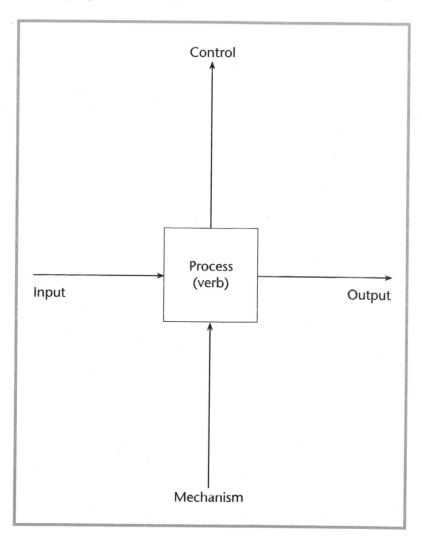

65

Market Analysis

When to use
When reviewing a company's strategy.

What you get
An overview of the product complexity relative to the market uncertainty which then enables you to consider the implications to the rest of the business.

Time
Approximately 1 hour's effort should provide useful insight. It can also be used as part of an in-depth strategy review.

Number of people
Can be used for analysis by a small group or for explanation to a large group.

Equipment
A wipe board or pen and paper. Ideally, the analysis will have supporting evidence.

Method

1 Draw out a four-box grid as shown in the example. Product Complexity refers to two factors. Firstly, the size of the bill of materials. Secondly, the sophistication of the technology in the product. Market Uncertainty refers to the predictability of sales volumes.

2 Discuss where all of the company's products (or product groups) should be placed on the grid.

3 Discuss the trends for movement of these products around the grid. Use arrows to show these movements.

4 Discuss the attributes of the company in terms of its infrastructure, people, facilities and image (a SWOT analysis could have been completed in advance).

5 Compare the attributes of the company to the requirements of the markets the products are in now and in the future.

6 Identify mismatches and brainstorm actions to address them.

Example
The example grid shows the four classifications together with examples of products and attributes that are normally associated with each. It also shows the key competitive factor for each sector.

> The axis can be given a scale if it helps.

Product complexity

	High	Low
High (Market uncertainty)	**Super Value** Examples: Aircraft and Oil rigs Example attributes: Strong design and development, IT systems, scientists, innovators, product creation ability. Key: Fitness for purpose	**Fashion or Jobbing** Examples: Jewellery and clothes Example attributes: Market vision, quick time to market, commercial innovators, product creation processes. Key: Time to market
Low (Market uncertainty)	**Consumer Durables** Examples: Cars and camcorders Example attributes: Flexible manufacturing, sytems engineers, team players, effective logistics and product supply. Key: Value for money	**Commodities** Examples: Food and drugs Example attributes: High productivity, lean logistics, systems engineers, frugality and tight cost control. Key: Price

Exercise
Map out modes of transport: trains, cars, bikes, skateboards, boats, etc. Compare the key competitive factors and example attributes to the example grid.

> Mobile phones were once Super Value products but rapidly became Consumer Durables.

Key points
Competing in more than one market type at a time forces compromises compared to a more focused competitor – jack of all trades, master of none. Different product types could be separated into different divisions, to protect branding.

Markets do evolve over time. To stay competitive a company needs to change its skills to meet the new market requirements or find new markets that suit its abilities.

◼ Additional comments

The grid can be completed at a number of levels, e.g. for industry in general or for a specific segment.

Placing a product in the wrong box initially will severely bias the rest of the analysis.

The tool is deliberately oversimplified, as there are obviously more than four types of industry. It works well in conjunction with Tool 15: Competitor Analysis. Use it to create understanding and generate debate not to provide definitive answers.

◼ Other information

Original concept developed by J. Puttick, University of Warwick.

Product complexity

high   low

Market Uncertainty

high

66

Product – Market Strategy Analysis

When to use
As part of a strategy development process.

What you get
A picture of a set of strategic options, which can be addressed in terms of products and markets.

Time
1–2 hours should provide a useful insight.

Number of people
3–12 people from different parts of the business will provide a useful basis for discussion.

Equipment
A wipe board or flipchart to capture the output.

Method
1 Draw up the four-box grid shown opposite.
2 In turn consider the products that your company or department offers or intends to offer and where they fit on the grid.
3 Take each quadrant in turn and ask yourselves questions, examples of which are shown below:
   – *Market penetration* – Do we have an advantage over our competitors? Can we sustain it and for how long? Will this provide growth? What could we do to increase market share? How fierce is the competition? How long can we continue in this quadrant?
   – *Product development* – Are the new products going to sell in the markets? What are the barriers to entry? Are there any new products that we could supply to existing markets? What is the competition like for new products? Have we got the processes right to deal with the new products? Are the new products going to make redundant any of the current product range? What happens if it doesn't take off?

   – *Market development* –How well do you know the market you intend to penetrate? How will those competitors currently serving the market react? Who besides you is likely to enter this new market? Existing competitors? Global competition? How will you know if it is not working and what contingency plans are in place?
   – *Diversification* – Is there an easier way of achieving growth with less risk? What can be done to minimise the risks? What actions have been taken to get up to speed with the new products and new markets?

Example
A health food shop.

	Products	
	EXISTING	**NEW**
Markets EXISTING	Low risk Health food to local community	Medium risk Complementary therapies to local community from current shop
Markets NEW	Medium risk Start up a new health food shop in a different area	Maximum risk Start up a complementary therapy shop in a new area

Exercise
Complete the grid and consider actions for some of the strategic options that are available for a bakery business.

Key points
This tool does not provide a golden answer, it provides a different perspective from which to view and consider different strategic actions.

It can also be used to look at the options available to grow and develop the business, and the risk implications of each.

■ **Additional comments**
This is an oversimplified tool that needs to be
used in conjunction with other strategy analysis
tools. Ansoff subsequently developed the model
further to incorporate a third dimension
'geographical growth'. For further information,
see the reference below.

■ **Other information**
The original concept developed by H. I. Ansoff
in 1965. Since then it has been developed
substantially further. For further information see
H. I. Ansoff, *The New Corporate Strategy*, Wiley,
1988.

PRODUCTS

	EXISTING	**NEW**
EXISTING	Market penetration	Product development
NEW	Market development	Diversification

Markets

67

Product Life Cycle

When to use
When analysing a company's product or service portfolio. An aid to strategy development.

What you get
A pictorial representation of the portfolio in terms of sales revenue on a timeframe.

Time
Assuming all of the data had been collated, 1–2 hours would provide useful discussion.

Number of people
3–15 is ideal; think about what you want to achieve from the session to determine whom you invite.

Equipment
Wipe board or flipchart, somewhere visible to display the findings and somewhere to capture the developments.

Method
1 Explain the concept of the product life cycle using the diagram opposite. A product is introduced, it goes through a growth stage when sales increase, it reaches maturity when the sales' increase is reduced, when sales begin to level it is in saturation, then when sales begin to reduce, the product is in decline. The timeframe for this alters with different products and companies, etc., but generally it is a cycle that most successful products go through.

2 For your business, agree a suitable timeframe to look at, run the time through to the present day. If wanting to predict a little into the future ensure that it is clearly understood as a prediction. Agree a suitable scale for the sales revenue (vertical) axis.

3 Place on the graph the product life cycles for the products in your business.

> You may need to break these down into product groups or create multiple charts for product groups.

4 Consider the implications of the picture you have of the business. Particularly cash and profit generation. Some example discussion points are included below;
   – Is it a balanced portfolio? That is does the portfolio have both cash consumers and cash and profit generators in balance?
   – Does it highlight any changes that may be needed with respect to strategy?
   – What are the implications to marketing, product development and business success?

5 Develop action plans to deal with the issues raised.

Example
A jeans company's product life cycle may look something like this:

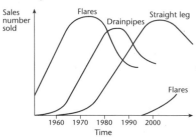

Exercise
Carry out a product life cycle analysis for a video shop.

Key points
This can be used on service offerings as well as products.

New products need to be started before the previous product enters decline otherwise there will be a dip in revenue. Too many new products introduced simultaneously can create a cash crisis.

This tool can be combined with Tool 50: Marketing Mix to develop marketing strategies for each stage in the product life cycle.

The value from this tool is from the discussions and actions that result from the development of the picture.

Additional comments

Not all products follow exactly that profile. Beware of seeing changes in sales and assuming they have entered another phase, e.g. a small downturn in sales could lead you to assume it has entered the decline phase and cause you to pull out of the market too early.

This is a very simplistic model, it is useful in terms of portfolio analysis, but be aware that there are a large amount of other factors that can alter the product profile.

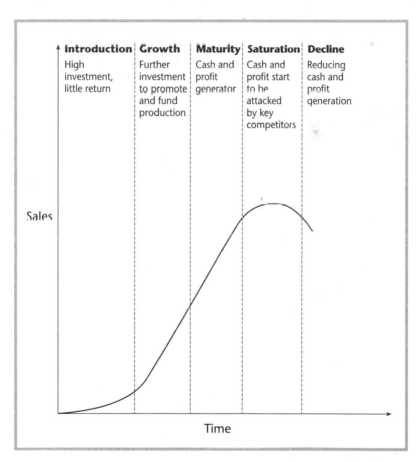

Introduction	Growth	Maturity	Saturation	Decline
High investment, little return	Further investment to promote and fund production	Cash and profit generator	Cash and profit start to be attacked by key competitors	Reducing cash and profit generation

Sales

Time

68

Quality Functional Deployment (QFD)

When to use
When comparing technical or operating characteristics of a product or service with customer needs.

What you get
A systematic translation of customer requirements to key design requirements of a product, process or service.

Time
2–4 hours for a simple chart and 2–3 weeks to capture the customer requirements.

Number of people
4–6 representing a range of disciplines including marketing, design and production.

Equipment
Pen, paper and a QFD grid.

Method
1 Determine who the customers are.
2 Gather data on customer requirements. Once QFD is established, this should be an ongoing process.
3 Using the QFD matrix (shown opposite), list customer requirements as WHATs and rate them from 1–10 (max) in importance to the customer. List design requirements as HOWs.
4 Go through each element of the grid, and evaluate the strength of the relationship between the WHAT and the HOW. If no relationship exists leave the element blank, or use the symbols for STRONG, MEDIUM or WEAK as shown in the table opposite.
5 The importance of each design requirement (HOW) can be numerically evaluated by multiplying the importance of each WHAT by the relationship factor (STRONG = 9, MEDIUM = 3, WEAK = 1, NONE = 0), and summing all the values for a HOW column.
6 This gives a numerical indication of relative importance and can be used to focus the design effort.

Example
Customer requirements for a budget airline are considered opposite.

Exercise
Create a simple QFD matrix for a petrol station.

Key points
Ensure you have the correct customers, e.g. a foodstuffs manufacturer should consider supermarkets, the purchaser and the consumer. Use questionnaires, focus groups, etc. to gather customer requirements. Don't get bogged down in detail, QFD gives a general view.

Pilot QFD as a process, to develop a full understanding of some of the practical issues. Be careful QFD can generate a lot of paperwork if not well controlled.

Additional comments
More complex charts may incorporate:

● *Correlation matrix*: characterises design requirement relationships, both positive and potential trade-offs.
● *Customer rating*: how does the customer perceive our performance against our competitors?
● *Object target values*: numerical design targets.
● *Competitive assessment*: technical assessment of how object target values rate against competitors.

This data is used to assess the current position in the marketplace, and again can be used to focus design effort on product or service offering.

A number of charts can be used to cascade the QFD through the business from design to manufacture, each stage forming the customer for the next.

Other information
For further information see: J. L. Bossert, QFD: *A Practitioner's Approach*, Quality Press, 1990; L. Cohen *et al.*, *Quality Function Deployment: How to Make QFD Work for You* (Engineering Process Improvement), Addison Wesley, 1995.

Customer requirements for a budget airline

WHATs \ HOWs	IMPORTANCE	Larger aircraft	Staff training	No perks (food, movie etc.)	Refit aircraft	Carry more passengers	More staff at check-in	Invest in in-flight entertainment	Internet booking	Invest in catering
Cheap ticket	9			◎		◎			○	
A good meal	2		○							◎
Leg room	5	△			△					
In-flight movie	3							◎		
Comfortable seats	4	○			○					
Fast check-in	8		○				○		◎	
Attentive stewards	1		◎							
Variety of destinations	6	◎		△		△				
Importance		71	39	87	17	87	24	27	99	18

Relationships

◎	9	Strong
○	3	Medium
△	1	Weak

Complex chart layout

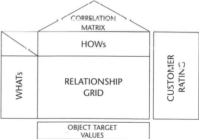

From the table, investment should be focused on an Internet booking and automated check-in as a key priority. Customers would rather have less 'perks' such as in-flight entertainment in return for cheaper tickets. Investment in larger aircraft rather than refitting the current fleet would also benefit the customer through reduced ticket prices.

69

Radar Chart

When to use
When you want to measure performance against requirements.

What you get
A graphical representation of actual performance in relation to ideal performance.

Time
The construction of a radar chart is fairly quick, however, it is important to get accurate performance information for each category, and it is this research that takes the time. The depth of research required will determine the time it will take to fully develop a radar chart.

Number of people
This will vary, however, it is important to get a wide variety of perspectives. More than 10 would be quite difficult to manage.

Equipment
Materials to gather and present the findings.

Method
1 Identify area for analysis.
2 Select and define the rating categories. These need to be specific to the area you intend to investigate. Tool 4: Brainstorming is a way of developing categories.
3 Define a scale for each of the categories.

> The measurements can be either objective or subjective.

4 Draw a large wheel on a flipchart with a spoke for each category. Label each spoke and add the scale. Ensure the scale is consistent, i.e. good is at the same end.
5 Research the category ratings to find out what level you are currently at and what level you need to be at.
6 Plot the findings on the chart.
7 Interpret and use the results. The overall ratings identify the gaps in each category, although give no indication of the importance of the category. It is important to focus on the biggest gap in the most important category.

8 Place the resulting chart in a prominent place. It can then be used as a way of monitoring progress.

Example
Exam results for a school.

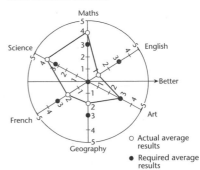

O Actual average results
● Required average results

From the radar chart it is possible to see areas where the school is strong and where it needs to focus resources to improve. In particular English is a subject that requires attention.

The technique can also be used to compare specific cases. For example, in this case we could have plotted on a 'child-by-child' basis to compare results and identify trends.

Exercise
Create a radar chart for successful business telephone enquiries.

Key points
This tool can be used in a number of different ways:

● *Internal analysis*: How are we doing in comparison to how we want to be doing?
● *External analysis*: What are our customers' expectations relative to what we are actually achieving or think we are achieving?
● *Multiple analyses*: Are there any trends apparent from a group plot of requirements? This could also help to identify blind spots.

■ Additional comments

As with all measurements consider the signals
that are being sent out. Are the results being
acted on or are we just measuring for the sake
of it? Are the measures appropriate to the
business goals and what we expect to achieve?

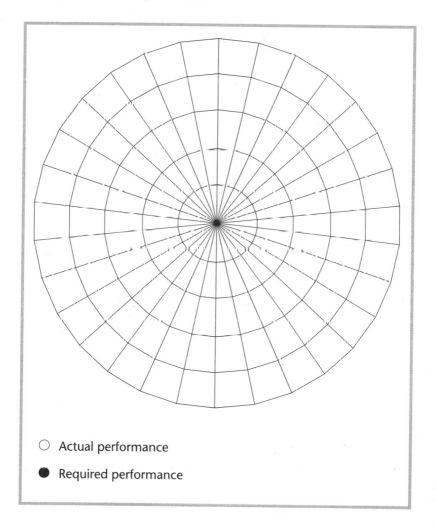

○ Actual performance

● Required performance

70

Risk Management

When to use

To asses the risks associated with the business or project either in steady state or through a period of change.

What you get

An assessment of the risks to the business or project so that appropriate actions to minimise the risks can be taken. Some examples being safety, product failure or call back, environmental, late delivery or failure to meet customer requirements, reputation, etc.

Time

1–2 hours to identify the risks and depending on the scale of the risk significantly more time to achieve an effective action plan.

Number of people

3–20 people. For best results, involve people with a good knowledge of the situation, the company or the project.

> *It is important to involve people who are able to assess both the probability and impact on the business.*

Equipment

Flipchart and or wipe board to draw up the diagram shown opposite and capture the developments.

Method

1 Brainstorm (Tool 4) the risks to the situation or project.
2 Position the risks on the grid shown opposite. The bottom axis shows the probability of the risk occurring and is set on a scale of 0–10, 0 representing an extremely low probability and 10 representing a very high probability. The left-hand axis shows the impact on the business or project if the risk does occur. It is set on a similar scale with 0 representing a low or negligible impact and 10 representing business or project failure.

3 The scale of the risk is calculated by multiplying the probability of the risk occurring by the impact that its occurrence will cause. The highest numbers representing the highest risk. It is possible to list all of the risks being faced by the business or project in order of priority.
4 Action plans need to be prepared against each of the high-risk categories in order to reduce the risk to a minimal level.

Example

Consider the risks for decorating a Christmas tree.

Risks: (a) Lights not working, (b) broken decorations, (c) no extension lead, (d) no one to help.

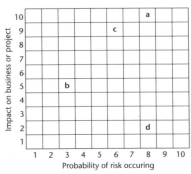

RISK	FACTOR	PERSON RESPONSIBLE/ ACTION
Lights not working	80	F.T. Test and fix before needed
Broken decorations	15	B.T. Check and replace
No extension lead	54	J.T. Locate or purchase
No one to help	16	B.T. Rally a team

N.B. In this case the predetermined acceptable level of risk was Factor 10 therefore all risks need to be acted on.

Exercise

Assess the risks of going on a diet.

Key points

It is not possible to eliminate risk totally and therefore it is important to make an assessment of the degree of acceptable risk. This normally requires the involvement of people quite high in the organisation, and if no one is responsible for business risk, it would be normal to involve a finance director.

Additional comments

Knowing the scale of a risk enables you to make sensible decisions about the effort and cost appropriate to reduce it or develop contingencies.

Don't think that risks are a bad thing. Businesses thrive by taking appropriately managed risks.

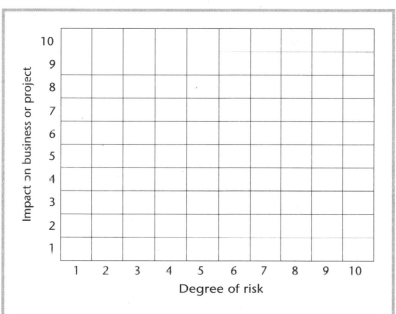

Risk	Factor	Person responsible/action

71

Road Mapping

When to use

When you are implementing plans to translate a vision into reality.

What you get

A graphic representation of your top-level plan showing key requirements for creating the future on a time scale.

Time

Depends on how much detail you want to explore. For an initial overview, 1–2 hours. For a more thorough plan, a few day-long workshops spread out over time will allow space to do additional research.

Number of people

It is important to involve key people from the business, along with both current and potential customers. It is important to get a thorough understanding of the business and the influences from different perspectives. Ideally no more than about 10.

Equipment

Somewhere to capture the outputs from the sessions.

Method

1 Ensure a common understanding of the aims and objectives of the road map, this will improve the effectiveness of the session and help people to interpret the map in the future.

2 Select the areas that you want to focus on for the road map, two to six areas are best, for example, market, products, business, technology, skills and knowledge. (If possible, use categories that are familiar to you.)

3 For each of the categories ask the question: Where do we need to be in 10 years' time? Capture this information on the right-hand side of the chart. It is important to have a wide range of perspectives, particularly those of the customer at this stage.

4 Then for each of the categories, work back, i.e. if that is where we need to be, what needs to be in place to make it happen? Continue along the timeline until you reach the present day. (This stage may require substantial research.)

5 When completed, simplify the road map onto one page and use the map to feed into the day-to-day plans and strategy.

6 Set plans for the next mapping session; it is important that it is a dynamic plan.

Example

See opposite.

Exercise

Develop a road map for your career.

Key points

Don't try and put too much information on the final road map – supporting research is important but can be contained elsewhere as a supporting document. Keeping the final one-page road map simple will increase its usefulness as a communication aid.

Don't use road mapping in isolation. It needs to be used in conjunction with day-to-day planning and future strategy planning. The road map is based on the current view of the future, which is continually changing. Keep it as a live document, which is reviewed at least annually so that it can directly feed into the day-to-day planning.

Be careful not to be too ambitious with the scope of the map. Don't begin by tackling the whole business, break it down into smaller sections.

Additional comments

Road mapping is a great tool for identifying the gaps in a journey to an end point, it does not tell you how to fill them.

Traditionally road mapping has been primarily focused around technology. However, the theory is applicable to a wide range of subjects from career development through to technology strategy development.

Other information

Thank you to Dr A. Clarke for her help in developing this tool. Other useful sources of information: Centre for Technology Management, Institute for Manufacturing, University of Cambridge. Sandia National Laboratories – Fundamentals of technology road mapping – www.sandia.gov.

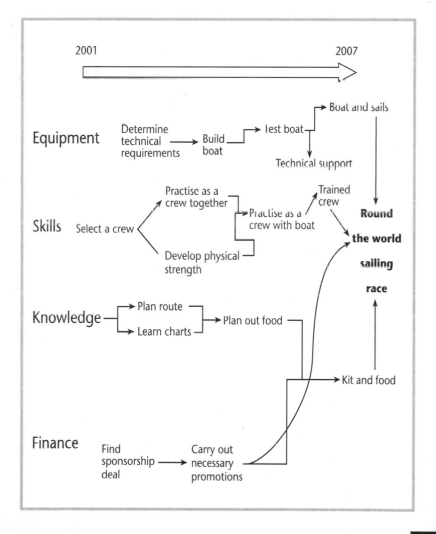

72

Run Chart

When to use
When studying results over a period of time.

What you get
A plot of the findings over a period of time making it easier to analyse.

Time
It will depend on the timeframe of investigation. This could be anything from minutes (when bacteria grows) to hundreds of years (if monitoring earth changes).

Number of people
It will normally take only one person to capture the findings. The setting up of the test, the analysis and action development as a result may take many more.

Equipment
Somewhere to capture the findings, graph paper or computer spreadsheet.

Method
1 Determine what is going to be measured, see Tool 52: Measurement Guidelines. Carefully consider what you intend doing with the findings, this should help you.
2 Determine how long a time period you intend to monitor and at what points there will be reviews.
3 Collect the data. Ideally collect between 20 and 30 data points to provide a suitable indication of what is happening.
4 Create a graph with a vertical line (y axis) and a horizontal line (x axis). On the horizontal line put time, and on the vertical axis draw a scale that will incorporate the range of results that have been collected over that timeframe.
5 Plot the data collected.
6 Analyse the chart. Look for emerging trends. It is also possible to plot on the chart the average of the measures therefore providing a base measurement from which to improve. By plotting the target on the same chart it provides a highly visible gap analysis.
7 Take appropriate actions.

Example
A run chart for wine consumption by one person over a two-week period.

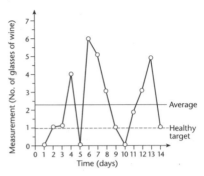

Exercise
Construct a run chart for your weight over a period of time.

Key points
Be careful to make sure it is real trends that are emerging, not just glitches. Control charts offer a statistical element to run charts, including moving averages and trend analysis.

The real value that comes from run charts are the actions that are taken to improve the situation.

Additional comments
Run charts offer no reasoning as to 'why' there maybe a trend emerging, it is important that the root cause (see Tool 10: Cause and Effect Analysis) is identified.

There are technical solutions (software) available to run real-time run charts. Look into specific applications for the most appropriate.

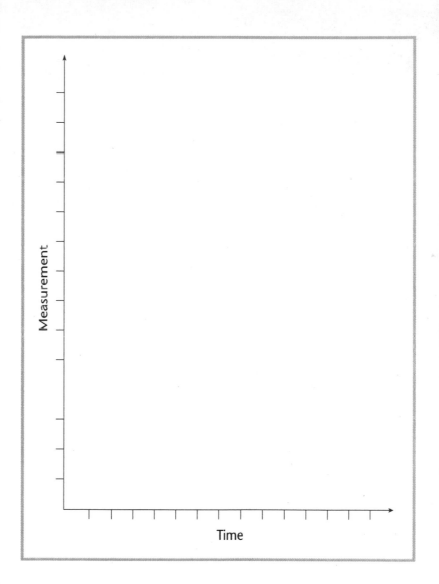

Run Chart

73

Scatter Diagram

When to use
When you need to display what happens to one variable when another variable changes.

What you get
An indication as to whether the two variables are related.

Time
The construction of the chart will take about 30 minutes. This does not include the time that is needed to collect the data to put into the chart.

Number of people
One person can construct the chart. The collection of data may require more than one person.

Equipment
Graph paper or other means of plotting data onto a graph.

Method
1 Collect 50–100 paired samples of data that you think will be related (ideally using a simple spreadsheet). For example, a person's weight and time spent exercising.
2 Draw the horizontal (x-axis) and vertical axis (y-axis) of the diagram. Label the x-axis with one variable and the y-axis with the other variable.
3 Place the required range of values on each axis. Highest values to the top and right.
4 Plot the data on the diagram. If you find that values are being repeated, circle that point as many times as appropriate.
5 Analyse the findings. To aid your analysis use the examples shown opposite.

Example
See opposite

Exercise
Complete a scatter diagram for the relationship between people's height and weight.

Key points
The scatter diagram enables you to identify a relationship between two variables, *it does not* identify if one causes another.

The examples given are based on straight-line correlations. However, there are many other forms of relationships that may be encountered. For example, $y^2 = x$, $y = x^2$ or $y = e^x$.

Additional comments
The main purpose of the scatter diagram is to help you understand a situation. It provides a quick and simple method of determining if there is 'something going on' for non-statisticians. You can then call in specialist statistical expertise as necessary.

Other information
It is possible to identify the exact degree of correlation, for further information on statistical tests, see M. J. Moroney, *Facts from Figures*, Penguin Books, 1990.

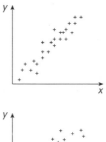

Positive correlation

As *x* increases, *y* normally increases.

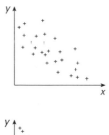

Possible positive correlation

As *x* increases, so does *y* but there may be other variables that are having a impact.

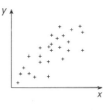

No correlation

A variation in *x* has no impact in *y* and vice versa.

Possible negative correlation

As *x* increases, *y* tends to decrease. It is likely that other variables are having an impact.

Negative correlation

As *x* increases, *y* normally decreases.

74

Scenario Planning

When to use
As part of a vision development programme.

What you get
A view of how different forces can manipulate the future in different directions. This enables you to mentally rehearse responses to key events.

Time
Varies depending on the scope and aims of the exercise. Assuming the background research is carried out beforehand, a one-day workshop should provide a useful outlook.

Number of people
A team of people from a cross-section of disciplines, and if possible a customer or other external perspective. More than 15 would be difficult to manage.

Equipment
Usual workshop materials, flipchart, wipe board, etc.

Method
1 Set the scene. Explain a little about scenario planning and why it has been chosen as an approach to take.
2 Identify the focal issues. This can be either broad, e.g. what will the future be for this market? or specific, e.g. how will technology change impact finance and admin in the future?
3 Identify the time horizon for the scenarios (normally somewhere between 5–30 years).
4 Identify the key factors or drivers for change, ideally concentrating on external issues over which an organisation has little control. For a framework see Tool 27: External Analysis (PEST). From your key factors, select those that are the most important to the business.
5 Agree on the scenarios that are to be developed (usually about 2–4 are used).
6 Develop the scenario detail linking it to the current state of the industry or world.

7 Discuss each scenario considering its plausibility, issues that it highlights and implications for today.
8 Select the more plausible scenarios and then either feed them into the strategy development process or use them to test the strategy for robustness.

Example
An example is shown opposite. It is very brief but serves to give an indication of the type and scope of a scenario planning session. For a more detailed example see P. Wack, 'Scenarios: shooting the rapids', *Harvard Business Review*, Nov/Dec, 139–150, or www.cio.com.

Exercise
Use scenario planning to address the issue of creating a future for small high-street shops.

Key points
Scenario planning acknowledges that the future is unpredictable and takes that into account by providing a number of different versions of the future. In contrast, most other strategic planning tools attempt to predict only one version of the future.

> There are no 'good' or 'bad' scenarios; they are purely a means to expand thought about the future.

It is essential that it is a participative process, as much value comes from the sharing of issues and perspectives of the future.

This is not something that can be done quickly by just anyone; it requires serious research, resource and commitment from the whole team.

This is not a one shot; it is something that needs to be revisited annually as the future keeps moving.

Additional comments
It is very advantageous to use an external facilitator to run the sessions, as this allows a broader perspective to be gained and enables creative suggestions to flourish.

■ Other information

Based on help from Frances O'Brien, University of Warwick. Useful references: P. Schoemaker, 'Scenario planning: A tool for strategic thinking', *Sloan Management Review*, Winter, 1995; G. Ringland, *Scenario Planning: Managing for the Future*, Wiley, 1998. See also: Institute for the Future (www.iftf.org).

Example – The future of the automotive market

Time frame: 10–15 years.
These are not predictions, just possible scenarios.

Key factors/drivers for change:

Political: Environmental legislation, zero emissions, legislation regarding disposal of vehicles (biodegradable), public transport becomes flexible, usable and the cheaper alternative, taxation increases on miles travelled

Note the varying likelihood levels of these factors

Economic: No longer feasible to afford to run cars, no longer feasible to be a niche player in the market, crude oil dries up, more 'easy to access' oil supplies found.

Social: Driving becomes a social misnomer, everyone works from home so families cut back to one vehicle per household, people living longer therefore more aged transportation requirements, lack of qualified engineers, environmental push towards minimising road travel.

Technological: New technology emerges to supersede current engine technology, new technology to supersede the car as a form of transport, personal flying machines made feasible, increasing technology offering solutions to prevent the necessity of travel.

Scenarios to be developed:

1 Combining the new technology to supersede the car as a form of transport with zero emissions legislation.
2 Reducing the need to be transported with more oil supplies found and no longer feasible to be a niche player in the market
3 More aged transportation requirements with legislation regarding the disposal of cars.

Each of the scenarios would be developed in more detail highlighting the implications to your business. A fun way to run this section is to divide the team into three groups, each taking one scenario, then bringing them back together to discuss their findings and share them with the group. It is at this point that most value is derived from the discussions. How these discussions are captured is key to ensure that any insights are effectively shared with the rest of the organisation.

75

Shared Values

When to use
At the start of any session that would benefit from a common understanding of the values held by the people around the table.

What you get
A discussion about values and an understanding of different people's perspectives resulting in a vehicle to produce company or team values.

Time
1–2 hours, depending on how long you let the discussions carry on for.

Number of people
For the exercise teams of 5–8 are ideal. Large groups can be subdivided accordingly.

Equipment
The story opposite and a flipchart to capture key learning points.

Method
1 Tell the group that you are about to read a very sad story. Ask them to listen and to note down the six characters on a piece of paper. Read the story (opposite) slightly dramatically laying some emphasis on the characters, the first time each is mentioned.

2 Now check that they have identified the six characters, i.e. Baron, Baroness, Lover, Gatekeeper, Boatman, Friend. Then ask them to list the characters in order of their responsibility for the death of the Baroness. Number one being most responsible and number six, least. This must be done quietly, on their own, with each one thinking out his/her own list. Allow about 3 minutes for this.

3 Divide the team into groups and ask each group to reach a *consensus* on the order of the responsibility of the characters 1–6. Before they start work, check that they understand what *consensus* means. Define consensus as an answer that every one of the group can understand and support. It is not dictatorial, nor does any form of voting or mathematical analysis achieve it. Allow them at least 15 minutes to do this.

> It is unlikely that any group will achieve consensus, challenge any group who think they have.

4 Re-assemble and get each group to give the name of who was most responsible and least responsible. Then ask them why it was so difficult. Suggest that would be possible only if they had agreed the rules first. These rules are the values against which the decisions were being made.

5 Discuss examples of the results that would come from a number of different value sets. This will depend on the audience's sensitivities. Some examples are given below:
   – What would be the results if we had used today's law in this country? This usually means No. 1 = Gatekeeper, No. 2 = Baron etc. Remember that no date was given in the story or place. Although it may have seemed like mediaeval England or Germany, it could have been yesterday!
   – What if we used the Ten Commandments? In these, 'Thou shalt not kill' and 'Thou shalt not commit adultery' feature.
   Point out how easy it is once the rules have been agreed. Then point out that a company's values are (or should be) the rules under which all decision making is governed.

6 Allow some time to develop meaningful values for your business or part of the business.

Exercise
Run the exercise with your family to determine the rules (values) that determine the allocation of household jobs.

This can be used at a number of levels, defining values/rules for a session through to the start of company-wide value development.

Although it will be a fairly painful process to agree the rules/values, it is important to remember the savings it will make in terms of time and energy from misunderstanding and conflict further down the line.

■ **Additional comments**

Different cultures, countries, religions all have different values, which will give different answers. Remember, there is no one right answer. The right answer is only true for the rules that form the foundation of the decision.

■ **Other information**

Source: D. Alexander, University of Warwick.

The Story

This is the story of a <u>Baron</u> *and a* <u>Baroness</u> *who lived together in a spacious castle. One day, the Baron said to the Baroness: 'I am going out for the day and will be back late. While I am away you must not leave the castle for any reason whatsoever. If you do, you will be in extremely serious trouble'.*

He then rode off.

After some time the Baroness became bored, so she left the castle and went to her <u>Lover</u>*'s house. After some time she awoke and realised it was getting late. She ran back to the castle and was just crossing the drawbridge when the* <u>Gatekeeper</u> *jumped out in front of her brandishing a sword.*

'Halt' he cried. 'The Baron has told me that if I was to find you coming back into the castle today I was to kill you.'

With that, she shrieked; ran back to the Lover's house and begged for help.

The Lover said 'I am sorry, but it's your own fault. If I help you, he will kill me as well. So clear off!'

The Baroness went back towards the castle and noticed a <u>Boatman</u> *on the moat. She had an idea and asked the Boatman: 'Would you row me to the back entrance of the castle so that I can get in?'*

'Gladly, my lady' he said 'but it will cost you £6.'

' I have no money with me at the moment', she said 'but if you take me over, I can go in and get some'.

'Oh, I am sorry, my lady,' he said ' but it's money up front or no crossing.'

So she went to a <u>Friend</u> *and asked to borrow the money.*

'No, I am sorry,' said the Friend, ' I if I do, your husband will kill me too.'

By now it was getting late and the Baroness was getting desperate. She returned to the drawbridge and there was no one around.

She decided to rush across, and, just as she thought she was home and dry, the Gatekeeper jumped out and ran her through with his sword.

Aaaahhh.

76

Six Sigma

When to use
When looking to further improve the quality of a product, process, service or business.

What you get
A quality target and plan to achieve what is effectively zero faults.

Time
It is an ongoing process.

Number of people
4–6 people should manage the process, incorporating the people who are involved in the process. Ultimately this may involve every employee in the business.

Equipment
No specific equipment is required, although process measurement may require measurement apparatus.

Method
1 Identify your product. (What are its characteristics?)

2 Identify your customers. (What do they require from the product?)

3 Agree with the customer the requirements you must satisfy. (How do the characteristics meet the customer's requirements?)

4 Define your processes. (What do you do to make the product meet these requirements? How can these be measured?)

5 Improve process quality to 'six sigma'. (An initial set of measurements will help to prioritise processes with the lowest quality.)

> Use tools such as 63: Process Control Charts; 86: Team Working and 24: Design of Experiments to measure and improve processes.

6 Mistake proof the process/product. (Reconsider the fundamental design.)

7 Continually improve the process.

Example
The method for a manufacturing process is:

1 Identify product characteristics that satisfy the customer.

2 Classify the characteristics to criticality, i.e. how important they are to meeting the customer requirements (see Tool 68: Quality Functional Deployment (QFD)).

3 Determine if the characteristics are controlled by a part or process.

4 Calculate the maximum allowable tolerance.

5 Determine the process variation.

6 Change the design or process to get a process capability that consistently meets six sigma.

Exercise
Create a presentation on six sigma using the approach.

Key points
Six sigma is a statistical term representing a distribution of six standard deviations about a mean. Sigma refers to the Greek symbol used to represent the standard deviation of a normal distribution (see opposite). This represents two defects per billion. In reality, a more achievable target of 3.4 defects per million is used based on a ± 1.5 sigma shift in the process mean.

Six sigma relates closely to Tool 63: Process Control Charts. Here the tolerance limits for a process are placed at three sigma. In six sigma the tolerance limits are placed at six sigma (see diagram).

The six sigma process benefits from the application of a range of quality tools.

Six sigma is as much about the philosophy of improvement as it is about the statistics.

The six-sigma target was set as a virtual zero defect rate, where investment in quality improvement would still be cost effective.

It is vital that the implementation of six sigma is driven from the top of the organisation.

People who are trained in six sigma have their level of training denoted by the karate belt system (black belt being the top).

■ **Other information**

Six sigma was initially developed by Motorola. For further information see F. Breyfogle, *Implementing Six Sigma: Smarter solutions Using Statistical Methods*, Wiley, 1999 and W. Kolarik, *Creating Quality*, McGraw-Hill, 1995.

Six sigma

The graph represents a normal distribution. This distribution represents the spread of any random variations in a product or process about its average value. On the chart below an upper and lower limit are set at 3 sigma. These represent the standard tolerance limits for a process being monitored using a process control chart. The shaded area represents the proportion of the product or process falling between these tolerance limits.

For this example, the target (average) output is expressed as a length (10 mm) and the tolerance bands are set at ±2 mm.

In a six-sigma process, the tolerance limits are pushed out to ±6 sigma. The measured tolerance values are not changed. It can be seen from the figure below that a greater proportion of the products are within the tolerance limits, i.e. the number of defects is reduced. In fact, only 3.4 parts per million now lie outside of the tolerance bands

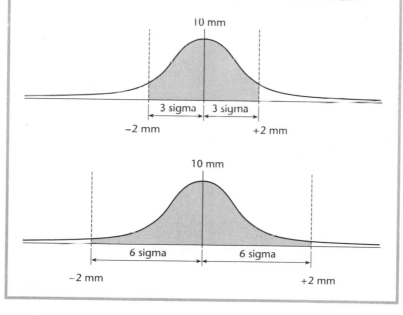

77

Skills Matrix

When to use
When looking to fill a position in a company, monitor personal development, or to assess the relative skills and weaknesses of an existing team.

What you get
A pictorial representation of people's skills and skill requirements.

Time
To develop the matrix categories will take 1–2 hours, the filling in of the matrix will require minimal time and can be updated on a continuing basis. However, understanding people's 'real' skills relative to other people's to provide a non-biased analysis may take quite a while.

Number of people
3–10 to develop the matrix. Involve people who understand the skills requirements.

Equipment
Somewhere to capture and display the matrix.

Method
1   Use brainstorming to identify the skills required to perform the required task(s).
2   Group the skills and select the 20 (or less) most important. See Tool 33: Forced Pair Comparison to help prioritise.
3   Place the requirements in a matrix on the top of the columns.
4   Down the left-hand side of the matrix label the rows with the applicants or the sample being analysed.
5   Fill in the matrix by following the row for each applicant and placing a symbol in each of the columns to indicate whether or not they possess each skill.
6   Once the matrix is complete it is possible to identify the person(s) most capable to perform the task, and potential skill gaps that will need to be addressed by the formation of development plans.

Example
Recruiting for a cricket team who require an all-rounder, there are four applicants for the position on the team.

	Catch	Bowl	Run	Field	Bat	Keep
John	X		X	X		
Will	X	X	X	X	X	
Chris				X		X
Paul			X		X	

Will provides the best all-rounder – the area that he is weak is keeping – this is an area that may require additional coaching. However, you only require one keeper in a team.

Exercise
Complete a skill matrix for the job role of the prime minister and consider the capabilities of the potential candidates.

Key points
This is a very useful tool when developing a workforce with a capability of flexibility. The matrix can be displayed in public and used as a quick and easy resource management aid as well as a training and development identifier.

It is also possible to use the matrix approach for a team, identifying the skills' requirements of the team and ensuring that the team covers all of the requirements rather than any one individual.

The skills matrix is very linear in this form; it is possible to add weightings to specific skills that are more important, or add another dimension by including how good they are at each skill.

If encouraging 'learning' throughout the organisation, the matrix could also be linked to remuneration.

Additional comments
If used for recruitment purposes, it is important to note that it only highlights someone's capability to do the job (skill fit). It does not provide any indication of a person's suitability to do the job (social fit). A behavioural analysis would provide a useful perspective in terms of suitability.

Other information

There are many behavioural analysis tools on the market; one of the more popular ones is Belbin's team roles, for more information see www.belbin.com.

Names ▼	Skills ▶

78

Solution Effect Analysis

When to use
When having agreed on a solution, you want to check that by solving one problem you don't cause another.

What you get
A structured way of checking the knock-on effects that the solution could cause.

Time
30 minutes to 1 hour should provide a fairly rigorous analysis.

Number of people
It is important to use a selection of people that were and were not involved in the solution stage. 2–10 is ideal.

People who are naturally quite cynical to changes are very valuable in these sessions.

Equipment
Somewhere to capture the findings, e.g. wipe board or flipchart.

Method
1 Ensure everyone is clear about the solution and place it on the left-hand side of the page.
2 Determine the major areas that will be affected and put them on the end of the bones.

To ensure a rounded perspective it is possible to use the areas of people, machine, methods and materials.

3 Then ask the question, 'What effects could this solution cause in the area of . . . ?' Ask this question for each of the areas on the end of the bones and capture the answers on the diagram.
4 Continue asking until the list of consequential effects has been exhausted.
5 Review the list considering which, if any, are the more potentially damaging.
6 Agree actions to address these potential effects and maximise the effectiveness of the solution. Alternatively, review the solution if it causes more problems than it solves.

Example
Problem: too much stress at work. *Solution*: gym membership.

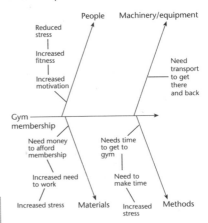

In this example it is possible to see that, if appropriate actions are not taken, then the solution could actually make the situation much worse. Alternative solutions may need to be considered or simple fixes implemented to cater for these knock-on effects, e.g. subsidised gym membership.

Exercise
Carry out a solution effect analysis for the problem of late pizza deliveries with the solution being to reduce the delivery area.

Key points
This is a simple visual technique. However, it does not guarantee the success of a solution, it merely opens people's eyes to other problems that could be caused by implementing a solution.

It is a particularly useful technique when introducing measures and controls. Measurement is often an area where the introduction of a new solution causes changes in behaviour.

Solution effect analysis is really a cause and effect analysis in reverse. Equally, it can be considered a simple graphical version of a FMECA analysis (Tool 28).

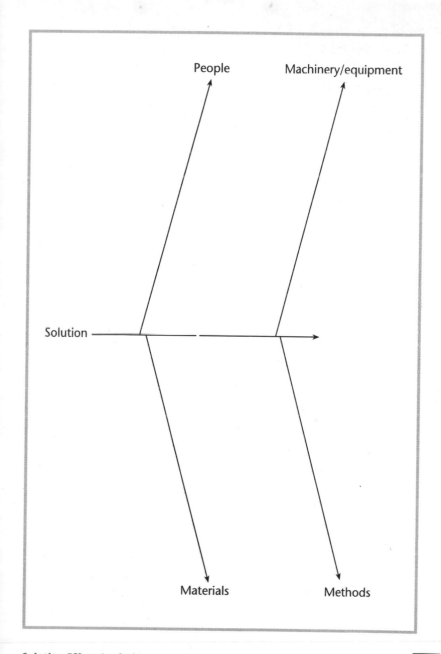

79

Sources of Innovation and Opportunity

When to use
When looking for new opportunities or ideas for innovation.

What you get
A framework to help you consider the innovation opportunities in your business.

Time
1–2 hours will provide a useful insight into the opportunities.

Number of people
5–17 is ideal, with a number of different backgrounds.

Equipment
A wipe board or flipchart to capture the output from the session.

Method
1 Talk through the theory of each of the seven sources of innovative opportunity that are detailed below, left, and consider for each of them the opportunities that exist for you and your business and make a note of them.
2 Prioritise the more important opportunities, see Tool 26: Effort Impact Graph or 33: Forced Pair Comparisons.
3 Create an action plan to explore the key opportunities further.

Example
Examples of each of the sources of innovation are below.

Exercise
Complete the exercise for a low-cost airline.

Source of Innovation	Description
Unexpected success or failure	Are there any areas that were surprisingly successful or failures, what are the opportunities that they bring to the surface?
Incongruities	Is there any difference between reality and what people believe it is? Are people interested in the product or the solution?
Process need	Is there an opportunity to improve current processes? Are there any processes that are over complex and inappropriate?
Industry and market structure	Are there any changes happening in the industry or the marketplace? e.g. legislation.
Demographics	Are there any demographic changes happening? e.g. age mix.
Changes in perception	Changes in people's perception of value of what is important etc.
New knowledge	Is there any new knowledge that provides new opportunities? e.g. technology.

Source of Innovation	Example
Unexpected success or failure	Unexpected success or failures of sports teams create a number of opportunities for their home towns.
Incongruities	People continuing to buy 'no sugar added' thinking there are no calories in the food. Opportunity to sell low calorie food.
Process need	Airports, why all the queuing? They know how many people need to go through each of the processes at which times; there must be a better way.
Industry and market structure	People are buying more and more from 'one-stop shops'. Opportunity to combine 'niche shops'.
Demographics	People are living longer – there are a number of implications to all industries.
Changes in perception	People are increasingly believing that green and environmental issues are important – green opportunities.
New knowledge	Consider the impact that the microchip has had on industry.

Key points

Don't overly force any of the areas, if no ideas or opportunities emerge, move on to the next one, you can always come back to it.

It is important that people are thinking creatively, it may be necessary to run some creative thinking warm-up exercises first, see G. Kroehnert, *100 Training Games*, McGraw-Hill, 1991.

Try to run step 1 in the fashion of brainstorming, keeping the points concise and holding all discussions of their appropriateness until no more ideas are forthcoming.

Additional comments

Some people may find that this tool adds too much structure to something that should occur naturally when you are looking for opportunities.

Other information

Based on P. Drucker's Seven Sources of Innovation, for further information see P. Drucker, *Innovation and Entrepreneurship*, Butterworth-Heinmann, 1999.

Source of Innovation	Ideas/Opportunities
Unexpected success or failure	
Incongruities	
Process need	
Industry and market structure	
Demographics	
Changes in perception	
New knowledge	

80

Stakeholder Analysis

When to use

When considering a change. It is particularly useful in terms of identifying who needs to be involved in the design and implementation of the change.

What you get

A list of people who will be impacted by the change which is being considered.

Time

1–2 hours should give you a comprehensive analysis. Note, this does not include time for subsequent actions.

Number of people

Ideally about five to enable a broad perspective to be gained.

Equipment

Wipe board or flipchart to capture the information.

Method

1 Clearly define the change or issue.
2 Brainstorm all of the stakeholders, i.e. people who the change or issue may affect either directly or indirectly.
3 Group the stakeholders.

> At this point, it is possible to see the scale of the impact that the change will have. It also gives an indication of the level of communication that will be necessary.

4 Then position them on the nine-box grid shown opposite.
5 You can now develop actions to facilitate the change that are focused on the specific groups. These actions can be prioritised depending on the group's level of influence and support. For example, the 'committed' with high influence will be worth getting involved to promote the change. No commitment with high influence will justify a significant level of effort to convince them that the benefits of the change outweigh their concerns.

Example

The opening of a new supermarket.

Stakeholders: customers, new shop owners, other shop owners, government, local community, schools, traffic controllers, police, potential employees, market traders, local MPs, land sellers, specialist shop owners, suppliers, delivery drivers.

When put into the grid . . .

Stakeholder Mapping

		No commitment	On the fence	Committed
Level of influence	High	Government	Local MPs	New shop owners
	Medium	Other shop owners Market traders	Suppliers Police	Land sellers
	Low	Specialist shop owners Traffic controllers Delivery drivers	Customers Local community Schools	Potential employees

Reaction of change

Exercise

Complete a stakeholder analysis for a new product line being introduced where you work.

Key points

The value in a stakeholder analysis is what you do with the collated information.
Communication and involvement of stakeholders in the appropriate way is often the make or break of change programmes.

■ Additional comments

Another way to use the analysis is with a group of people to do a role play of each of the groups of people concerned. This enables you to get a much richer understanding of how the change looks from their perspective.

It is worth noting that people with 'no commitment' to the change, influential or not, may have some very real reasons for their behaviour. It is always worth investigating these reasons, as you may find them useful in order to prevent problems before they happen.

■ Other information

Further information can be found in J. Burgoyne, 'Stakeholder analysis' In C. Cassell and G. Symon (eds), *Qualitative Methods in Organisational Research*, Sage, 1994.

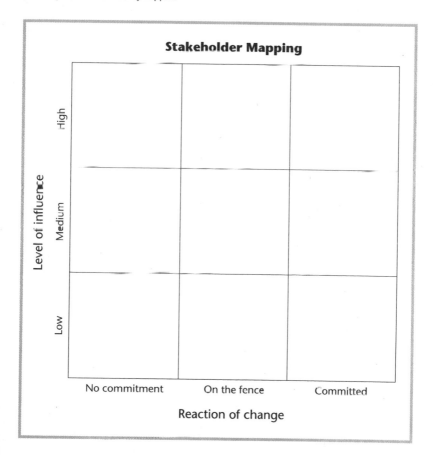

81

Strategic Planning

When to use

When designing a 1–3 year plan for the company, division, department or project, or when you want to make a significant change to the positioning or performance of any of the above.

What you get

A fully evaluated road map and action plan that will take you from the present position to the desired future if it is achievable, or a route to a less ambitious desired future if it is not.

Time

To create a fully evaluated and bought-into strategic plan will normally take about 3 months.

Number of people

A selection of people who will have to deliver the agreed strategic plan. Involve sufficient numbers of people at all levels in the organisation to secure buy-in and commitment. The actual numbers involved will depend on the size of the organisation, the degree and the complexity of change.

Equipment

An effective strategic plan will draw on many of the tools in this book. In addition you will need somewhere to develop and distribute the plan.

Method

Presented here is a high-level guide to the preparation of an effective strategic plan.

1 Assess where you are now, consider both internal and external positions. Some other tools, which may help, are: 83: SWOT Analysis; 27: External Analysis (PEST); 3: Benchmarking; 57: Order Qualifiers and Order Winners.

2 Ensure you have considered external elements such as is the market growing or declining, are more competitors entering, what are the barriers to entry, what is happening to the product life cycles?

3 Consider what strengths new market entrants might bring.

4 From understanding where you are now, consider what a desirable future would look like for your operation.

5 Clearly articulate the desired future and write it down in the simplest form possible. Tool 71: Road Mapping would help here. Test the clarity by involving employees at all levels within the organisation. Be prepared to modify it from the feedback.

6 Establish what is missing from the current operation to achieve the desired future. Realistically assess the timescale cost and resources to deliver the missing elements together with different options for delivery.

7 Prepare a clear evaluated plan to incorporate details of the elements, timescales and milestones. In addition, prepare the business case, see Tool 17: Creating a Financial Business Case.

8 Gain corporate approval for the plan together with the commitment to the funding and resources.

9 Prepare a detailed work package breakdown (Tool 94) of the task and get buy-in from the work package leaders. Involve all who have to understand and deliver elements of the plan and make sure that they fully understand the strategy and desired future.

■ Example

Regard the preparation of the strategic plan as the preparation of a route on a map from one town to another. To prepare such a route you need firstly to know where you are, and determine where you need to go, a map of the area, you need to know where towns A and B are on the map, the roads, the landmarks and towns between the two towns. Then you need to know how you are going to tell if you have got there. Whilst this may seem obvious, it is essential that all involved understand it.

■ Exercise

Create a strategic plan (simplified version) for moving house.

■ Key points

The strategic plan for the company is a culmination of the strategic plans for all divisions, departments and projects. Therefore, if your plan is to be a subset of the corporate plan, it must be fully compatible with it. A strategic plan needs to be reviewed regularly.

Getting buy-in across the organisation is key. Consider carefully people's involvement and how you present the plan to others.

■ Other information

For further information see L. Goodstein *et al.*, *Applied Strategic Planning. How to Develop a Plan that Really Works*, McGraw-Hill, 1992.

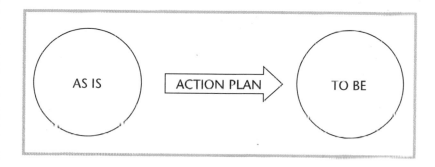

82

Strategy Framework

When to use

When developing or reviewing a strategy.

What you get

A view of where you want to be, where you are now and key elements that need to be taken into consideration when developing action plans to get there.

Time

Assuming you have all of the information present developing the strategy should take about a day. Making it happen will take substantially longer.

Number of people

10–15 people ideally from different parts of the business.

Equipment

Somewhere to capture the developments.

Method

1 Set the objectives. Consider how you want to compete. And therefore what you need from your business (or part of the business) to enable you to compete more effectively.

2 The objectives should then be rated by customer needs. Tool 57: Order Qualifiers and Order Winners is good for categorising these. For increased detail a nine-point importance scale is shown below.

	1	Provides a crucial advantage with customers – main thrust of competitiveness
Order winning objectives	2	Provides an important advantage with most customers – it is always considered
	3	Provides a useful advantage with most customers – it is usually considered
	4	Needs to be at least up to good industry standard
Qualifying objectives	5	Needs to be around the median industry standard
	6	Needs to be within close range of the rest of the industry
	7	Not usually considered by customers, but could be
Less important objectives	8	Rarely considered by customers
	9	Never comes into consideration by customers and is unlikely to ever

3 Judge achieved performance, list all of the objectives and place them on a nine-point performance scale as indicated below.

1	Consistently considerably better than our nearest competitor
2	Consistently clearly better than our nearest competitor
3	Consistently marginally better than our nearest competitor
4	Often marginally better than most competitors
5	About the same as most competitors
6	Often within striking distance of the main competitors
7	Usually marginally worse than main competitors
8	Usually worse than most competitors
9	Consistently worse than most competitors

This requires an in-depth knowledge of your competitors.

4 Plot each of the objectives on the importance/performance chart shown opposite.

5 Develop action plans to move elements into the 'appropriate zone'. Focus initially on the elements 'urgent action' and the 'improve zone'.

Strategy Framework

Example

In this example, the key areas for immediate action would be improving product quality and on-time delivery.

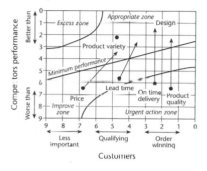

Exercise

Complete the framework for your business.

Key points

Moving customers' perceptions is also an option.

Although originally designed for a manufacturing environment, the framework is transferable to other parts of the business.

Additional comments

There are a number of strategy frameworks, this one provides a thorough customer-focused approach.

Other information

Source: N. Slack *et al.*, *Operations Management*, Pearson Education Ltd, 2001.

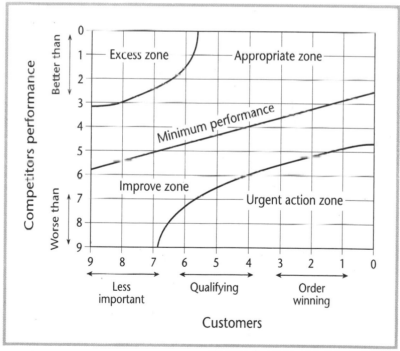

83

SWOT Analysis (Strengths Weaknesses Opportunities and Threats)

When to use
Either to start or sum up most types of review sessions.

What you get
A snapshot of a situation highlighting areas of strength and weakness.

Time
Half-an-hour can provide reasonable results. However, the summary can be left visible, revisited and added to over the course of a project.

Number of people
From one to many although, for practicality, 2–10 is most useful.

Equipment
A large wipe board to record results. Additional materials for brainstorming may be necessary (see Tool 4: Brainstorming).

See the hints for Brainstorming.

Method
1 Draw out a four-box grid as shown in the example.
2 Get the group to suggest pertinent strengths, weaknesses, opportunities and threats. It is often useful to use brainstorming techniques for this stage.

Generally speaking, strengths and weaknesses will be features from within your business or department. Opportunities and threats will tend to come from outside.

3 Repeat the process until the group seems to be running out of ideas.
4 Discuss the list. Considering actions to maximise the strengths, compensate for the weaknesses, utilise the threats and optimise the opportunities.

Example
Here is a SWOT analysis for the idea of producing this book.

Strengths	Weaknesses
We know lots of tools. We have practical experience of using them. We know how to teach the use of tools.	We have no experience of producing a tool book. We have no facilities to publish.

Opportunities	Threats
People we work for are asking for a tool book. There are no simple to use, practical cover-all tool books.	Someone might write one before us. Conflicts with our consulting business.

Exercise
Complete a SWOT analysis for you personally in your job.

Key points
The important thing is to raise issues for discussion. Putting them in the right box is far less important. In reality, trying to place them is just a means of sparking debate.

Do not stop people from recording issues on the grid. If it's important to them, it's worth discussing.

■ Additional comments

There are two primary methods of filling in a grid. The first is to work through the four headings one at a time. The second is to allow issues to be generated and then discuss where on the grid they should be placed. The first method tends to work better when people are not familiar with the tool. The second approach is better when you have a group that have already worked together successfully. It can be useful to review the original grid periodically, especially during a project, to see what has changed.

The tool can be dangerous if it is not used honestly. There is little point in not taking into account the reality of the situation, good and bad, if you don't the resulting actions will be damaging.

It is also useful to complete a SWOT for your competitors and then compare, looking for areas where you can gain competitive advantage.

■ Other information

Concept originally developed by
H. I. Ansoff. For further information see:
H. I. Ansoff, *Corporate Strategy*, Penguin, 1987.

Strengths	Weaknesses
Opportunities	**Threats**

84

Systems Thinking

When to use

When needing to analyse a complex system or situation, or when considering different solutions to a problem to see the potential outcomes.

What you get

A view of the whole system and the interrelationships between elements of the system.

Time

Dependent on the scale and complexity of the system that is being looked at. 1–2 hours should provide an overview.

Number of people

Involve a selection of people who are involved with the system to provide a rounded knowledge base.

Equipment

A wipe board or flipchart to capture the developments.

Method

Systems thinking encompasses a large number of methods, tools and principles. What follows is a brief introduction to one of the basics: causal loop diagrams.

1   Clearly define the start point or problem.
2   Consider the effects that this leads to. Use sentences such as 'this in turn causes . . . or would cause . . .'. Map these on the diagram linking them with arrows and ensuring that the direction of impact is indicated.
3   Continue to ask and note the consequential issues until ideas dry up.

> Brainstorming would provide a good place to start – consider the process as a continuum cause and effect analysis.

4   Now revisit the loops and check that they are true, sufficient and complete.
5   Select options or actions to create a desired outcome.

Example

See opposite.

Exercise

Use systems thinking to review the problem of poor performance of a football team.

Key points

Systems thinking is based on the premise that everything is connected in some way, exploring the connections provides a useful way to get a holistic picture of the situation.

Causal diagrams can be used to both analyse current situations and test options in terms of solutions.

There are no right and wrong systems diagrams – there are a number of different options that each have their own benefits and consequences. The important thing to note is that things rarely happen in isolation, therefore it is important to consider the wider ramifications of changes. You may end up with a number of interconnecting loops.

Causal feedback can be both reinforcing (amplifying the start point), as seen in the example, and balancing (limiting), e.g. a thermostat.

There are a number of common systems behaviours. These are called systems *archetypes*. The archetypes can be useful to help build and test models about the system.

Other elements contained within the discipline of systems thinking are cybernetics, chaos theory and Gestalt theory.

Additional comments

This is most effective when used to analyse or predict process or system failures. Tools 29: Fault Tree Analysis and 10: Cause and Effect Analysis are more effective for physical failures such as establishing the cause of high defect rates.

For most situations it is beneficial use systems thinking to truly represent the complexity and interrelatedness of factors.

A useful and practical guide into the key
elements of systems thinking, and particularly
the archetypes can be found in P. Senges, *Fifth
Discipline Fieldbook*, Nicholas Brealey, 1994.
It also provides a very comprehensive reference
list for exploring areas in further detail. Also see
The Systems Thinker, Pegasus Communications
Inc. Cambridge, MA, November, Vol. 5, No. 9
and Vol. 6, No. 5, 1994.

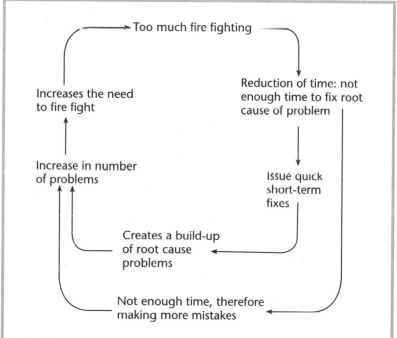

Reading the systems diagram, it is possible to
see a reinforcing loop.

There is too much fire fighting, which
causes there to be insufficient time to fix the
root cause of a problem. With insufficient
time people install quick short-term fixes to
problems which adds to the build up of root
cause problems, which leads to more overall
problems, which leads to more fire fighting
making the situation worse.

Somehow the cycle has to be broken, if
things are going to change, a possible
solution may be to create a team to address
root causes of the backlog of problems, this
will then create some space so that in the
future, there is the time to deal with the root
causes rather than issuing quick fixes for the
symptoms.

85

Team Selection

When to use
When selecting a project team.

What you get
An approach to selecting a balanced and complementary team.

Time
To agree the approach to team selection should take between 2–4 hours.

Number of people
2–3 people from different perspectives, close to the subject matter and if possible a customer (possibly internal customer).

Equipment
Somewhere to capture the output of the session.

Method
1 Identify the skills necessary for the team (see Tool 77: Skills Matrix).

2 Identify the types of people needed on the project. (Some of the behavioural analysis tools that are available have suggestions on this, for example Belbin suggests that a balanced team needs nine different team role types to provide a balanced team.)

3 Identify possible candidates for the team (this can be done in a range of ways from getting people to volunteer or nominating people; each have there own merits and drawbacks).

4 Analyse the candidates both in terms of their skill fit and their behavioural fit.

5 The ideal team size is between 7 and 15, select a team within these guidelines based on the analysis from the previous stages.

6 Consider how that team would work together (this too is offered by some of the behavioural analysis tools). Will they 'get on' with each other, are they compatible? Do they have a range of behavioural styles? Are they a balanced team? Alter the selection according to the findings, bearing in mind that skills can often be developed whereas behaviours are very difficult to change.

7 Finalise the team.

8 Enrol the team. At this point it would be valuable to run the team working session to enable the team to begin working together effectively. As part of the enrolment process, ensure roles, responsibilities, values, objectives are clarified and clearly understood by all.

Example
Selecting a team to sort out the garden.

Skills: strong, dig, knowledge of weeds and plants.
Behaviours: enthusiastic, self-directing, analytical, finishers, ideas.

Name	Strong	Dig	Knowledge	Enthusiastic	Self-directing	Analytical	Finishers
Bob	✓	✓		✓	✓		
Dave	✓	✓				✓	
Pauline			✓	✓	✓	✓	✓
Emma	✓	✓			✓	✓	
Matt	✓	✓		✓	✓		✓
Jerry	✓	✓		✓	✓		✓
Andy	✓	✓	✓				

In this case, the team members would be Bob, Pauline, Emma, Matt and Jerry. If we needed an extra member, it would be Dave because he has the behavioural requirements and can easily be taught about the difference between weeds and plants.

Exercise
Consider the elements that would need to be taken into consideration when selecting members for a pop group.

Key points

There are behaviour analysis tools on the market that can help with the behavioural aspects, see Tool 86: Team Working.

Involving the behavioural elements, significantly improves the effectiveness of the team.

If you are involving people of different levels in the organisation in the same team, be sure to set clear ground rules to manage this.

Communication in the team will be key, see Tool 48: Leaning Styles.

Commitment is also an area of importance, see Tool 18. Creating Commitment.

Additional comments

There is *no* perfect team. There *are* successful teams who work at it.

Other information

There are many behavioural analysis tools on the market. For further information on Belbin see www.belbin.com.

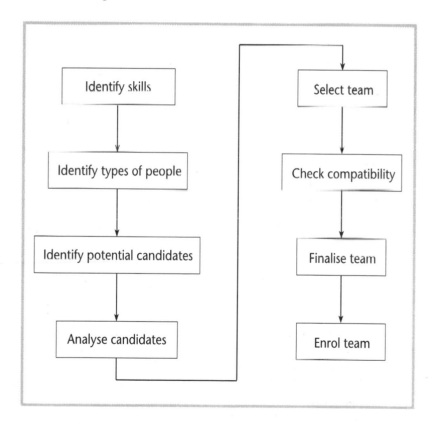

86

Team Working

▇ When to use
When looking to enable a team to work more effectively together.

▇ What you get
An understanding of individuals' needs and requirements in a team environment. Thus providing a base from which to improve working together.

▇ Time
At least one day to develop and foster a team-working environment. Improvements will be on a continuous basis.

▇ Number of people
Ideally 5–15. Fewer than 5 gets too personal and more than 15 leads to subgroups forming.

▇ Equipment
Somewhere to display information and capture the outputs of the session.

▇ Method
1 Do some preliminary work to get a clearer understanding of the individuals in the team. This could take the form of a behavioural analysis such as Belbin team roles, Myers Briggs, Target Training International, or could be simply asking some questions, for example: What are the five main things that you look for in an effective team? What are the five main things that stop this team from working effectively? What strengths and weaknesses do you bring to the team? What are the team's strengths and weaknesses? The key thing is to build a picture of the individual and the team.

This information then needs to be collated and presented at the start of the session as a discussion point. Most of the behavioural analysis tools have a facility to provide a team report.

Getting away from the office as a team can also substantially help the team's development.

2 Develop a vision of what effective team working means to the team. For example, name some examples of exceptional teams. What elements made them exceptional?

3 Identify issues, gaps, areas for improvement given the understanding of the individuals and the team.

Be careful of sensitivities surrounding the sharing of this type of information; ensure it is a safe environment and that people know that it will only be used for the purposes of improving working together.

4 Identify actions to move the team towards the vision of effective teamwork.

▇ Example
See opposite.

▇ Exercise
Run through the process with your family.

▇ Key points
This tool is working from the point where a team is already selected, this could be due to a number of reasons such as organisational structure or skills mix. Ideally a team would be selected to maximise their ability to work successfully together, see Tool 85: Team Selection.

Much of the benefit of this tool is from creating a forum for discussing behavioural issues, which there is little time for in everyday work.

It will be important to enrol the help of an impartial facilitator for the session to ensure an objective approach is taken.

The session must not be used to victimise and pick on individuals. The focus must be on: What do we need to do to work together better?

The real benefit of the process is that it provides an opportunity to discuss the issues that affect team success in a safe environment.

Additional comments

This tool provides only a picture of the opportunities to improve the team dynamics, it does not identify skills gaps, see Tool 77: Skills Matrix. Using this tool and the skills matrix will provide you with both the team's capability and suitability to achieve their aims.

Be careful, the approach depends on the honesty and openness of the people in the team. Ensure that this is encouraged and not abused.

The real benefit of the tool is to discuss the issues that affect team success in a safe environment.

Other information

There are many behavioural analysis tools on the market, for examples see, www.belbin.co.uk, www.tti.co.uk.

A SAILING TEAM

Name	Strengths	Weaknesses	Actions
Ian	Knows a lot about the boat	Fails to communicate with parts of the team	Consider ways to improve communication
Steve	Does as told. Accurate and enthusiastic	Will not take control of situation. Worries	Work nearer Cath. Gain an understanding of the root of the worry
Jerry	Good coach	Often too busy looking after other people to do his own jobs	Focus in on one person to help per race
Tim	Natural leader. Keeps the peace	Finds it hard to take decisions	Clearly give him the role of leader. Understand the reasoning behind the hesitation in decision making
Cath	Stable, calm	People see as being too laid back	Work nearer Steve
Andy	Takes control	Tries to do everything	Give an area to manage. Work on understanding why he feels he has to do everything

This example provides a summary of the exercise and highlights some of the areas for potential focus.

87

Technology and People

When to use
When introducing new technology into the business. Ideally use at the beginning of a technology introduction planning process.

What you get
An awareness of the relationship between technology and people, which can be used to develop a balanced approach to its introduction.

Time
Spend about 2 hours working around the framework. This needs to be kept in mind throughout the whole technology introduction.

Number of people
1–20 for the development of what it means in your context. It can be used in bigger groups as a communications exercise.

Equipment
The matrix opposite, and somewhere to capture other outputs from the session.

Method
1 Draw up the matrix shown opposite and discuss the fundamental principles which it highlights, i.e. that a more successful outcome is likely if the people element of the technology introduction is focused on, even if the technology isn't perfect. (Take about 10 minutes to make sure everyone understands.)
2 Brainstorm all of the issues that would make the people element of the technology introduction successful.
3 Brainstorm all of the elements that would make the technology element successful.
4 Develop an action plan and appropriate measures to incorporate the results from steps 2 and 3 to ensure a balanced approach to the technology introduction.

Example

People	Technology
Training	Specification
Education	Connections
Communication	Infrastructure
Involvement	Maintenance
Support	
Processes	

Exercise
Consider the elements necessary for the successful introduction of a personal computer at home.

Key points
The technology could be software or hardware.

It may be worth considering the possibility that if you get the people element of things right, the need for the new technology may be diminished or even removed.

A balanced approach between technology and people is required from the planning stage to beyond the implementation. The people elements need to be acted on as well as considered.

Additional comments
This tool is more of an awareness tool than anything else; the philosophy will need to be fully embraced to really benefit.

Human nature drives us to focus on the tangible technology side of the introduction. It is worth considering the potential waste that could result from not focusing on the people side of things.

Other information
Source: S. Turner, Towards Successful Technology Introductions, Executive Summary, Engineering Doctorate, 1998.

	PEOPLE	
	Wrong	**Right**
TECHNOLOGY **Wrong**	Disaster	Excellent
Right	Poor	Fantastic

88

Thought Capture

When to use

When trying to understand a subject and the way it relates to other issues. It is particularly useful when trying to stimulate creativity.

What you get

A pictorial map of a subject.

Time

Depending on the nature of the subject anything from 10–60 minutes.

Number of people

It is normally done on an individual basis but can be used for larger groups – see key points.

Equipment

Somewhere to capture the diagram.

Method

1 Write down the main subject in the centre of the page.

2 As ideas or issues associated with the subject come to you, capture them using a few words or a picture on the diagram.

> Don't worry about the pictures not being very good; it's about capturing the essence not winning a drawing competition.

3 Show the connections between subjects as appropriate. You can use different colours for linking subject areas.

4 Continue to think of links, ideas, issues and thoughts and capture them on the diagram. Allow your brain to freewheel around the subject.

Example

The uses of thought capture.

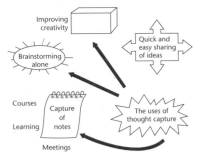

Exercise

Using the blank page opposite, summarise the last book you read using the thought-capture technique.

Key points

Thought capture is best done using hand drawings and sketches. This tool can be used to both capture and create.

This is a great tool for spicing up solitary brainstorming sessions, but is also good for capturing the essence of workshops. It is possible to hire artists to capture workshops in this way; these can be fantastic as they provide a simple pictorial stimulus for each attendee.

Additional comments

It helps to capture the ideas in creative ways, as it often sparks different ideas. It will also help to trigger the essence of the issue when you come back to the diagram.

Do not assume that everyone will understand your diagram; different things create different connections for different people. It is important to not over complicate the picture with words. The more you use the technique the better you get at it.

This is a quick start approach to thought capture; the technique can be used in a number of different ways at a number of different levels.

Other information

Thought capture is an adaptation from mind mapping™ and dendo diagrams. For further information on mind mapping®, see Tony Buzan, *The Mind Map Book – Radiant Thinking*, BBC Books, 1993; Ingemar Svantesson, *Mind Mapping and Memory*, Swan, 1989; Nancy Margulies, *Mapping Inner Space*, Zephyr Press, 1991.

Thought capture

89

Time Based Process Mapping (TBPM)

When to use
When you are looking to improve efficiency and effectiveness throughout a business.

What you get
A visual time-based representation of business processes in terms of value and non-value adding activities.

Time
To do the research will depend on the scope of the project and the accessibility of the information. The construction of a high-level TBPM will take 1–2 hours.

Number of people
To achieve the desired improvements you should involve all of the process' stakeholders at appropriate times. However, the initial research and development of the current map will require 2–10 people, depending on the size of the process being mapped.

Equipment
Large area to capture the findings and draw the map, wipe board or paper on the wall.

Method
1 Investigate the process that you have chosen to map. Sketch a flow diagram of this process to show the linkages and dependencies of the subprocesses within it.
2 Next, get data on the time that it is taking real jobs to pass through each of the subprocesses and the time spent waiting between them.
3 Using the information from above, calculate the total time that the overall process consumes from beginning to end. It is worth comparing this theoretical time to the actual times that jobs are taking. This ensures that you haven't overlooked any stages in the process.

4 Plot the TBPM as per the example. The top axis will show the total time from start to finish of the process. The left-hand axis will show the various subprocesses within the overall process. For simplicity these should be listed in the order that they are performed.
5 Draw in process bars to represent the typical start and finish time for each subprocess. (Ideally use average times, however, in some cases it may be important to show the maximum and minimum times.)
6 Highlight the value-adding subprocesses. These can be identified by the following: Does it alter the nature of the product or service in a way that the customer would want? If yes, then it's value adding. If no, then it's non-value adding. Examples of non-value adding time are rework, waiting, storage and queuing.
7 Label on the TBPM the value-adding time and breakdown the non-value adding time into its key areas.
8 Calculate the value-adding time as a percentage of total time. This will be used as a stake in the ground for the measurement of future improvements.
9 Consider all of the elements of non-value adding time and create an action plan to minimise if not eliminate the non-value adding time.

Example

Getting through an airport for a plane.

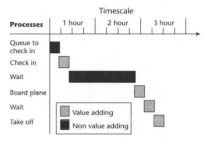

Timescale

66% of the time in the airport is non-value adding.

Areas for improvement would be in the queue and the initial waiting time. N.B. the second wait is considered value adding; this is because it is time for safety checks and the customer has paid for a 'safe journey'.

Exercise

Develop a TBPM for your day at work.

Key points

Not all non-value adding is 'bad', i.e. some transportation may be necessary to get the product to the customer. What TBPM does is highlight areas of opportunity for improvement. It is important to question *why* is it necessary and how can non-value adding be minimised.

It may be worthwhile getting an external facilitator to help with TBPM, as it helps to have an external perspective to question the norm.

Some people add greater detail to the TBPM by using different colours to show different types of non-value adding activities.

Other information

Based on concepts in I. Gregory and S. Rawlings, *Profit from Time*, Macmillan Business, 1997.
Diagram reproduced with permission of Palgrave.

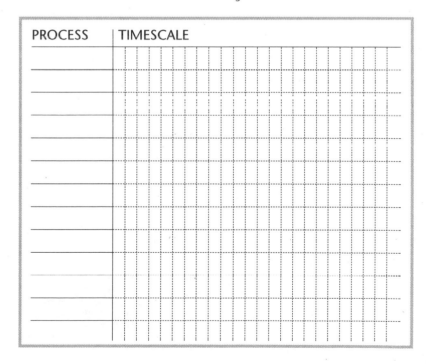

Time Based Process Mapping (TBPM)

90

Time Management

■ When to use
When needing to use your time more effectively.

■ What you get
A series of actions that will help you to manage your time more effectively.

■ Time
It will take just over one week of elapsed time, and about 2–3 hours of total time.

■ Number of people
One, although it will probably involve other people when you get to the action stage.

■ Equipment
Recording sheet as shown opposite.

■ Method
1 Begin by understanding exactly how you spend your time. Do this by monitoring what you do for 5–7 days. You can either fill in the recording sheet opposite or create your own.

2 Analyse the findings on your recording sheets.

   Mark against each of the tasks if they were tasks that you *must* do, *should* do or *like* to do. Calculate the percentage split of your time spent doing each of these types of tasks. Consider if this is an appropriate split, and also what ideally the split should be.

   Calculate the percentage of time that is spent working on tasks given by different people. Consider the implications of the split. Is it mainly coming from your staff? Are they too dependent on you? The boss – are you being used as a personal assistant? Consider what would be an appropriate split for you?

With each of the tasks listed, think about whether it could be delegated. If it could, to whom? What would need to happen to enable these tasks when they are required in the future for the delegation to happen automatically? If it couldn't be delegated, why not? What would need to change to enable it to be delegated? Which of these tasks 'ideally' should be delegated?

3 Create an action plan. In each of the areas highlighted, develop a list of actions to improve your time management.

   > At this point it may be beneficial to involve your boss or colleagues to discuss possible improvements.

4 Review how you are spending your time 1–2 months later by going through the process again. Look for areas of success and failure, and other aspects that could be improved further.

■ Example
On analysing the findings from the record sheet, it initially appeared that 98% of the tasks could not be delegated. Further investigation revealed that there were people who these tasks could be delegated to with a little explanation and training. This has meant that of the initial list of tasks 52% of them are now delegated allowing more time to do additional tasks.

■ Exercise
Complete the exercise for yourself.

■ Key points
If you are reading about this tool, you think you need to improve your time management, having read it you think you haven't got time to do it! It does require investment upfront, but the benefits far outreach the investment. Also, you could always get someone else to 'shadow' you for a week and fill in the record sheets for you. This would be a great project for a student or someone who was interested in understanding more about the business and the job role.

During the monitor and analysis stages *do not* make excuses, this was an abnormal week, etc. you may have lots of abnormal weeks.

Feel free to add other columns to the recording form and do other analysis in different areas that are specific to your business.

This tool relies fundamentally on honesty, don't let the fact that you are recording what you are doing alter your behaviour.

Based on concept developed in: M. Pedler *et al.*, *A Manager's Guide to Self Development*, McGraw-Hill, 1998.

Time Record Sheet

Time of day	Task/ Activity	Duration	Where work came from	Comments

91

Visioning –
The Future

When to use
At the beginning of a strategy development or road mapping programme.

What you get
A definition of the company's vision and purpose.

Time
1–3 hours will provide a fairly comprehensive picture.

Number of people
A selection of key people from across the business. 5–15 people will produce a rich vision.

Equipment
Wipe board, paper or flipchart, somewhere to capture the output from the session. Post-it™ notes and pens.

Method
1 Determine the timeframe for the exercise. Use a timeframe that is appropriate for your business, for example, 3 months for a project to 5 years for a business plan.
2 Set the scene: now, today, it is the end of that time frame and you have created the most successful business you can imagine.
3 Individually write on sticky notes your own answers to each of the questions in turn (example questions shown below). After the team has had a chance to write down their own ideas for the first question, all of the Post-its™ are placed on the wall, read out and discussed. The main points from the discussions need to be captured (there are no right or wrong answers). Then take each question in turn in a similar manner.

- Who are the stakeholders of this successful company?
- How do they perceive us as a company?
- How are we making money?
- What external factors are affecting us?
- What makes us special?
- How do we compete?
- What does the organisation look like?
- What are our major strengths?
- What does it feel like to work for the organisation?

> You can also add your own questions.

> As you go through the questions people's ideas and visions will draw together.

4 Pull out all of the key elements of the vision session and refine them down to one sentence which everyone is happy to work towards and buy into. Write in the present tense.
5 At this point you can either use it as part of a strategic plan (Tool 81), a road mapping exercise (Tool 71) or a business excellence framework (Tool 9). Or, come back to the current year and look at the organisation as it is today and answer the same questions. Then create an action plan to deliver what is missing to create the future vision.

Example
See opposite.

Exercise
Use the process to define a vision for your career.

Key points
You can run the specific exercise detailed above on your own, *do not* develop a company vision on your own, it is important that other people have an input to its development. It is important that everyone's input is given the same respect.

It is possible to tie this exercise into Tool 1: Analogies, i.e. using an analogy to help the visualisation of the future.

This session often highlights big differences in people's ideas of where they want the business to go. It is important that these are made to come out into the open, and agreement reached on a way forward.

■ Additional comments

The visualisation of the future may be very hard for some people. If people are having difficulty bring the timeframe back a few years. This tool relies heavily on good facilitation.

■ Other information

A practical guide to vision development can be found in P. Senge *et al.*, *Fifth Discipline Field Book*, Nicholas Brealey, 1994. For inspiration of good visions see J. Collins and J. Porras, *Built to Last*, Century, 1996. Also see T. Goss, *The Last Word on Power*, Piatkus, 1996.

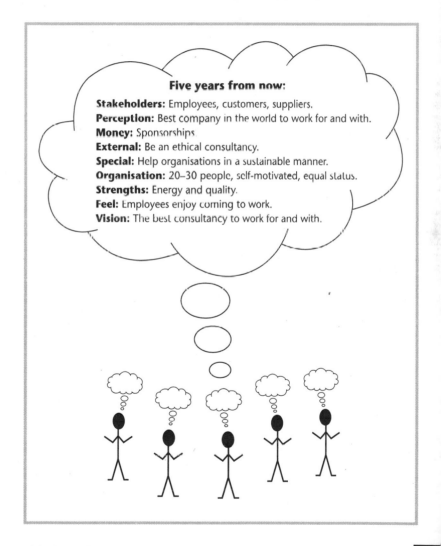

Five years from now:

Stakeholders: Employees, customers, suppliers.
Perception: Best company in the world to work for and with.
Money: Sponsorships.
External: Be an ethical consultancy.
Special: Help organisations in a sustainable manner.
Organisation: 20–30 people, self-motivated, equal status.
Strengths: Energy and quality.
Feel: Employees enjoy coming to work.
Vision: The best consultancy to work for and with.

92

Vital Few Analysis

■ When to use

When you need to identify the 'vital few' or the most serious problems in a situation. It is also called Pareto analysis, the 80/20 rule and ABC analysis.

■ What you get

A visible representation of what the major issues are and an estimate of the magnitude of the benefits.

■ Time

This will vary depending on the availability of information.

■ Number of people

This can be done solo, although it will rely on people believing the data they are presented with, therefore it may be important to involve them in the data collection.

■ Equipment

Somewhere to capture the data and present it in a graphical format.

■ Method

1 Identify all possible problems in a particular process.

2 Collect data on these problems. You can measure how frequently these problems occur and/or the costs associated with the problems.

3 Construct a table listing all of the problems from the greatest to the smallest (see the exercise example).

4 Plot the data on a chart (see Tool 38: Histograms), placing the item with the greatest cost/incidence in the furthest left column, then the second-most important, etc.

5 Calculate the percentages of each of the items against the total then plot the cumulative percentages on a line graph.

6 Draw a line from the 80% point on the *y*-axis, drawing this line down to the *x*-axis will indicate the few issues which are causing 80% of the effects.

7 Focusing your efforts on this small number of issues will address the bulk of the problem.

■ Example

The diagram shows you how the analysis normally looks.

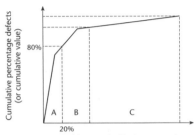

Problems ranked by frequency of occurrence, value or type

Those items in the A category are the most important to tackle, as 20% of the issues are causing 80% of the problems.

Some examples:

20% of customers account for 80% of turnover.
20% of product range account for 80% of turnover.
80% of costs are tied up in 20% of business.

■ Exercise

Create a vital few analysis for the problem of too much scrap based on the data shown below.

Reason	Cost of scrap (£)	% of total	Cumulative %
Material fault	78,150	78.6	78.6
Machine breakdown	15,275	15.3	93.9
Setting error	3,500	3.5	97.4
Operator error	1,250	1.4	98.8
Tool breakage	1,150	1.2	100.0
Total	**99,325**	**100.0**	**100.0**

Key points

Vital few analysis is useful in a number of different areas including major problem identification, inventory control, forecasting, finance, marketing and personnel.

It can also be used to prioritise solutions and to show progress of the before and after situation.

Additional comments

This tool is heavily reliant on the quality of information fed into it; therefore it is worth checking the accuracy of the information.

It is important to note that it is not always a simple split, and to question the reasons for the distribution before acting on it.

Other information

Concept developed in A. Smith, *The Wealth of Nations, Penguin*, 1982. For further information on application see Richard Koch, *The 80/20 Principle: The Secret of Achieving More with Less*, Nicholas Brealey, 1998.

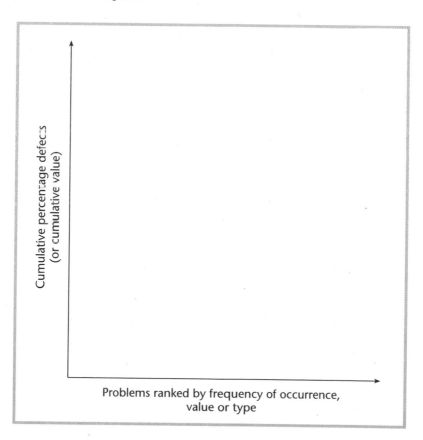

Cumulative percentage defects (or cumulative value)

Problems ranked by frequency of occurrence, value or type

93

Waste Minimisation

When to use
When looking to improve the business by minimising waste.

What you get
Focus for action around seven key areas where waste is often found.

Time
To analyse the situation 1–2 hours. However, the real value comes from carrying out the actions and removing waste. This will be an ongoing process.

Number of people
It is important to involve the people who will be affected by the improvements. This may require subgroups to be formed.

Equipment
Somewhere to capture and monitor the areas of waste within the business.

Method
1 Explain the benefits of removing waste, i.e. improved quality, effectiveness, productivity and morale.

2 Explain the seven common sources of waste as detailed below:

Defects are expensive in both time and material. Take time to understand the root cause of defects and prevent them happening again.

Over production costs through tying up resources and by hiding problems. Make what is required when it is required.

Inappropriate processing increases the cost of a product. Ensure that the processes are streamlined and that you use the right tool for the job.

Transportation does not increase the value of the product, it draws heavily on personnel and equipment and provides opportunity for loss and damage. Ensure that all transportation is kept to a minimum.

Inventory costs money to hold and risks becoming obsolete. Aim for minimum stocks.

Waiting is non-value adding and as such is a waste of time and money. Think about what else can be done with this time or how scheduling could be improved.

Motion can waste time and money. Always try to minimise the motion in a job.

3 Look at each type of waste in turn and identify example areas within your own business where waste can be minimised. Capture the results on the chart.

4 Take each of the areas of waste minimisation in turn and put some actions in place to begin the process of waste removal. Identify who is going to be responsible for the improvement process.

5 Set review meetings in place to share knowledge and review the progress of the waste minimisation exercise.

Example
For a bakery: see table opposite.

Exercise
Consider areas of waste in your business.

Key points
There are other areas of waste that are also very important such as waste of human potential, waste of knowledge and waste of energy. It is also worth considering these when looking to improve the business.

The benefits that come from this tool are from the actions that are taken subsequent to doing the analysis.

Be careful that improvement projects don't lose sight of the bigger picture. You don't want improvements in one area to cause problems in another.

Other information
Adapted from the original concept, which was developed by Toyota's chief engineer, Taiichi Ohno.

TYPE OF WASTE	AREA FOR FOCUS	ACTIONS	PERSON RESPONSIBLE
DEFECTS	Production	Research extent of problem	Greg Hall (Baker)
OVER PRODUCTION	Sales outlet	Measure end-of-day stock levels	Amy Dexter (Shop assistant)
INAPPROPRIATE PROCESSING	Whole process	Review current process	Ian Little
INVENTORY	Production	Review raw material stock	Greg Hall
TRANSPORTATION	See above	See above	See above
WAITING TIME	See above	Consider more effective use	All employees
MOTION	See above	Review layout	All employees to offer improvements

TYPE OF WASTE	AREA FOR FOCUS	ACTIONS	PERSON RESPONSIBLE
DEFECTS			
OVER PRODUCTION			
INAPPROPRIATE PROCESSING			
INVENTORY			
TRANSPORTATION			
WAITING TIME			
MOTION			

94

Work Package Breakdown

When to use

Whenever you have a project to manage where it is essential that it is delivered on time and within cost budgets.

What you get

Early warning of potential cost or time overruns.

Time

Dependent on the project complexity, nominally 1–10 days.

Number of people

A team of the people responsible for the delivery of the major project elements.

Equipment

A project plan.

Method

1 Take the project plan and break it down into manageable elements in terms of time, cost and deliverables.

> It is essential that the person who is accountable for delivering the elements of the project agree to the timescales for their part.

2 Take each of the elements in turn and establish someone who would be accountable for the delivery of each element. If this cannot be done, consider further breakdown or amalgamation of elements.

3 Once accountable people for each of the elements are identified, agree the task, timescale and budget for their elements with them.

4 The overall project then needs to be reviewed with the revised timescales and costings to ensure it still meets the overall requirements. Place milestones in the project plan to highlight each element's deliverables, date and cost.

5 Set up a performance monitoring system to overview progress and take timely corrective action and, or renegotiate modified timescales and budgets with other accountable people in the project.

Example

See opposite.

Exercise

Take a map of part of the country. Select two places on the map, some distance apart. Plan a journey between the two using an average speed of 25 mph on ordinary roads, 50 mph on A roads and motorways or freeways. Take the cost per hour of running your vehicle at £10. Determine the lowest cost and shortest time route, with cost being the primary driver. Establish five milestones along the route, where you are able to define the cost and timescale targets that are necessary to achieve the overall journey targets.

Key points

Note it is essential that a community spirit of mutual trust is developed between the accountable people to make this work. Therefore it is preferable for them to be involved in the original planning process, so that the overall desired outcome is clear in everyone's mind.

This technique is enhanced significantly if incentives are attached to the achievement of the work package cost and timescale targets. However, agreeing the targets with the people concerned becomes more difficult. In turn, this may encourage senior management to involve those who have to deliver at the bidding or contract stage, through which buy-in is relatively automatic.

Additional comments

It has been found that this approach whilst fundamentally common sense has produced significantly improved project management. However, it is no substitute for a good project plan, and just provides a vehicle to make it deliverable.

Other information

Source: F. Turner. Try the following for other information on project management: S. Baker and K. Baker, *The Complete Idiot's Guide to Project Management*, Alpha Books, 2000; K. Posner, *The Project Management Pocket Book*, Management Pocket Books, 1998.

Project to organise party for 7 September

Project elements	Accountable person	Agreed timescale (weeks)	Agreed budget	Due date/ Milestone	Issues arising
1. Invite people	Angela	4	£30	1 July	
2. Finalise numbers	Angela	2	£10	14 July	
3. Research venues	Gordon	2	£20	15 June	
4. Book venue	Gordon	1	£2000	21 July	
5. Details to attendees	Caroline	1	£20	1 September	Need replies from Angela
TOTALS		10	£2080		

Project Plan

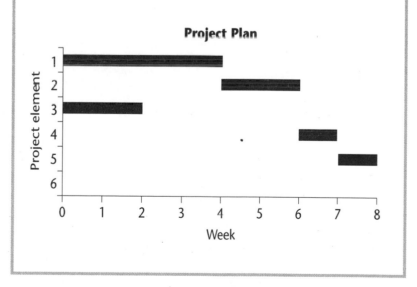

Index